POETRY NOW

BETWEEN THE LINES

Edited by Kerrie Pateman

First published in Great Britain in 1995 by
POETRY NOW
1-2 Wainman Road, Woodston,
Peterborough, PE2 7BU

HB ISBN 1 85731 423 9
SB ISBN 1 85731 428 X

FOREWORD

Although we are a nation of poetry writers we are accused of not reading poetry and not buying poetry books: after many years of listening to the incessant gripes of poetry publishers, I can only assume that the books they publish, in general, are books that most people do not want to read.

Poetry should not be obscure, introverted, and as cryptic as a crossword puzzle: it is the poet's duty to reach out and embrace the world.

The world owes the poet nothing and we should not be expected to dig and delve into a rambling discourse searching for some inner meaning.

The reason we write poetry (and almost all of us do) is because we want to communicate: an ideal; an idea; or a specific feeling. Poetry is as essential in communication, as a letter; a radio; a telephone, and the main criteria for selecting the poems in this anthology is very simple: they communicate.

Faced with hundreds of poems and a limited amount of space, the task of choosing the final poems was difficult and as editor one tries to be as detached as possible (quite often editors can become a barrier in the writer-reader exchange) acting as go between, making the connection, not censoring because of personal taste.

In this anthology over two hundred and thirty poems are presented to the reader for their enjoyment.

The poetry is written on all levels; the simple and the complex both having their own appeal.

The success of this collection, and all previous *Poetry Now* anthologies, relies on the fact that there are as many individual readers as there are writers, and in the diversity of styles and forms there really is something to please, excite, and hopefully, inspire everyone who reads the book.

CONTENTS

THE PHOTO

When you and I were children and we had our childhood dreams
we imagined life before us, and our love together seemed
to us to last forever in our house of innocence
but children don't know everything, my dreams died one Sunday night
when I saw her in your arms in a lemon pool of light

I saw you both together but you didn't sense me there
and the gap between us widened as the moonlight touched her hair
I was looking at a photo, taken thirty years ago
but the woman in your arms in the photo decades old
was the woman who was standing in the darkness and the cold

My mirror image smiled and her face was like the sun
when it rises in the morning and the day is new begun
I have that look on film, it is thirty years old too
with your arm around your best man on the left hand side of you

Now you and I are older whereas she is just a child
she smiles on you a little like the way I used to smile
thirty years ago, in our house of innocence
when you and I were children, I realized most dreams didn't last
I thought that we were different, but we are buried in the past

Sarah Outhwaite

SUMMER WITH ANNA

Summer with Anna and her friends
It has some being some truth.
If it was anything I had known
Tell me now.

Samira shone in parks
I photographed her on the swing.
Anna gave me something
Craved for but not answered.

Once had grass twisted in my hair
With another sang from Lewis Carroll.
These seem so distant
Writing from the tower block of wasted dreams.

This summer I can only say
Anna
Anna
Anna

S T Pearson

MASTER MARINER

Four days out in the Pacific -
bad weather -
under pressure to deliver -
then some one taken ill on board.
A difficult decision.
Alone in darkness
with the sea your mistress
under you
the cargo
shifting in the hold.

Irene Evans

THE VELVET SKY

Velvet black night,
Melancholy knowing,
Shout at the moon!
But wait . . . as it fades behind velvet,
Plunged into blackness, emptiness.
Ceiling of shadows,
Look up into the ink,
Islands in the universe.
Points of light.
As in existence, all is not dark,
Starlight in the vault of the heavens.
Radiant fairylights scattered across the sky.
Mood lifts, realisation of enormity.
Namesakes of the gods, realm of legend,
Pleiades, Cassiopia, rise of Orion, galaxy of Andromeda.
Wandering star, I am not alone.

D E Thomson

SCHOOLDAYS

Listen to the quiet our teacher mused.
It foretells the gathering storm.
Oh for the comforting squeak of chalk
on blackboard. Scratching out the wisdom
of a World we never knew.
Our lives were duffle-coated Batman capes,
Dinky car races and British bulldog
with its explosive collapse.
We would too soon know the storm that life unleashes
on unsuspecting little creatures.

David A Caven

BITTER HARVEST

The young graceful almond, so slender and fair.
Finds a tangle of ivy entwined in her hair.
Ignoring the fine cords of bright tender hue,
They bathed in the sun the long summer through.
As the ivy gripped tighter embedding in deep,
A strange lassitude o'er the almond did seep.
While almond fruits ripened to a rich hue of gold,
The ivy clung harder to tighten her hold.
And all through the winter while host was asleep,
The ivy grew stronger extending her creep.
But when spring awoke the innocent fruit tree
Found her energy sapped by the vigorous ivy.
She rattled bare branches, no leaf did she bear
Bedecked by the ivy, weighed down with her care.
Their destiny fixed at the time they were sown,
Together they died, by the axe they were hewn.

Beware for the seedlings while still young and tender.
Their lives can be blighted without a defender.
Be watchful and ruthless, and crush under foot
the forces of evil which gnaw at their root.

Gauntlett Blake

4

PROPERTY GUIDE

House for sale the sign proclaims,
Some have numbers, others names.
Des res waiting for a buyer,
ritzy, glitzy for high flier.
Terrace, modest, on three floors,
stripped pine features, panelled doors.
Semi-detached, a family's dreams,
rooms with scope for colour schemes.
A solid cottage dwelling standing
on a corner, are you handing
ownership to caring buyer,
this cosy home with open fire.
Country house to suit a gent,
'Society' will see he's lent
a tidy sum to live in style,
he's reached his goal, just see him smile.

Marion Rose

OUR MEETING

When we meet your smiling face looks
at mine searching for recognition of
that longing love held deep within;
then eyes meet minds and lock themselves
gently together to form a bond of
belonging that only we two share. A
shimmering haze descends and wraps
its cloak of special happiness safely
around us closing out the whole world,
leaving us to linger in our thoughts.
Hearts beat louder, hands meet, bodies
touch - oblivion.

Maureen Collinge

WINTER

Pinched, like a homeless orphan
Waif with a begging bowl,
Cold and withdrawn, yet pleading
Tearing my very soul.
Wild with her tatters blowing,
Numb is her spirit within,
Sombre her eyes, all shadows,
And limbs that are bare and thin.
Sad that we shun her presence -
Pass by, collars up, heads down.
Doors closely shut against her
Whether in country or town.
Sometimes she's cloaked in white velvet,
Bejewelled in frost's bright splinter.
Such fantasy though is but fleeting.
Poor unloved and unwelcome Winter!

Patricia Farley

UNIFORMITY

Don't they look sweet, the little ones,
In their smart new uniforms,
Isn't it a heart-warming start to the day,
- the reception class in their blue and grey?
Mine isn't 'sweet', she uses her head,
She wears what she chooses
Instead.

K Levey

LOVE LIVES IN INFINITY

Far away on the mountains of
darkness and space
Where the annals of time disappear,
There's an ordinary sanctuary
wound up in lace
Where afraid lurks the maker of fear.

In obscurity neighbouring the
mountains of time
On which birth, death and age integrate;
There's a universe causing the
substance of rhyme
And a universe making its fate.

There's a universe causing the
wonders of joy,
And a place where alone lives esteem,
There's a land where the urge dwells
to kill and destroy,
And a land which is built on a dream.

By the eyes of the hills and the
eyes of the sea,
Where the men sing and dance all the day,
There is even a place where the
pure air is free
And a place where for pure air you pay.
And within the wide circles of
life's hidden gold
There's a place for your mind and your freedom
There's a place for the young and a
place for the old
All encased in a marvellous kingdom.

But despite all these fables of
lands far away,
All these fables of kingdoms above,
There is nowhere an evening and
nowhere a day
There is nowhere a kingdom for love.

Martyn Wynn

THE FOX

Sneaking through the undergrowth on the edge of town,
Snorting, sniffing, looking up and down,
Creeping round the farmyard, moonlight all aglow.
Wary of the sheepdog, tired of all the snow,
Winter with its vice-like grip, frost on every bush,
Ground as hard as iron, water turned to slush.
Chickens settled in the shed, geese are in their pen,
Stealthily he makes a move, stopping now and then.
In the shed the feathers fly, dust is all around.
A victim falls, nowhere to hide, left bleeding on the ground.
A light goes on, a shot rings out,
He leaves without a fuss,
A dozen feathered friends or more left lying in the dust.
A second shot rings around his ears, he doesn't stop at all.
Nearing home he's comforted by his companion's call.
Safe and warm now underground, his quarry were all lost,
The farmer on the other hand begins to count the cost.

R Parker

GIVING IT AWAY

Why do we humans require trappings.
Make life such a complicated feat.
When all the other species,
Live to eat to live to eat.

Our lives could be so very simple.
As we in other races see.
With concessions on possessions.
Not just, this is all for me.

The constant need to travel.
When life is shelter and a meal.
If only guns had been invented.
We could have shot the man, that made the wheel.

Life could be a bowl of cherries.
If we let our greed just slip.
Why go for the fattest berry,
When you only need the pip.

People are what really matters.
Should your life be long or short.
For the things that give life purpose.
Are not for sale, cannot be bought.

Make a play for satisfaction.
Get away from greedy strife.
Pleasures shared just to remember.
With a loyal and loving wife.

T A Napper

THE BARGAIN BUCKET

'Roll up! Roll up!
Fifty pence a go
What special gift can you find
In the bargain bucket?'

I took off my jacket
Rolled up my shirt sleeve
And plunged with carefree abandon
To the bottom of the barrel

'What is it?'
I thought
As I removed my ornate package
Wrapped in silver paper
Reflecting the sunlight

I hurriedly opened it
And found to my surprise
An emotion
Repressed and backing into the corner
Like a frightened pup

I thought
'That will come in handy,
I'll keep it in a box, by the door,
In the hope there'll be a rainy day.'

Francis McFaul

POETIC GUISE

I keep you locked inside my head
an image real and concrete
playing the waiting game
testing my loyalty
if I put you into words
will the critics tear you apart
or will you simply let me down
a figment of my imagination

I need to know before I give you form
will you give me satisfaction
or will you merely leave behind
an empty shadow by my side
in my heart you are my dream
in my mind you become reality
yet I must banish you from my head
before you take over my life

Patricia A Clark

ON LISTENING TO KISMET

The garden was walled.
Nectarines, ripe and hanging
Gave fragrance to the morning air.
Fountains sprayed, catching gold coins of light.
Rippling and quivering, in amongst the plants
Where colour glimpsed the sky.
Minarets peered everywhere
As the voice of the muezzin
Fused into every pin point of space
Forcing wakefulness into morning,
Where dreams pervade the very stones.
The call to prayer is clear and strong
Spinning on the scented air.

Margaret Gibian

HIGH DEPOSIT, BUT RE-USABLE . . .

Raymar lay quite still, quite naked, yet he felt no cold,
Shrouded by transparent canopy of simu-gold,
His wounds, horrific, yet no scars at all would seal his flesh,
But heal he would, and quickly, for the wars would start afresh,
Robot attendants hovered silent, micro-circuits glowed,
His time was drawing near, and fear across his dark eyes showed,
The clock, implanted in his cortex at the age of three,
Passed silent pulses to his spinal block and set him free.

Pain surged along his limbs, and splattered colours in his brain,
A thousand lances tore his mind, put sanity to strain,
'Hold on, hold on!' his memory screamed; 'It's like this every time,'
'No, no, much worse,' his psyche replied and sank to depths sublime.

The air was dark and cool when Raymar next opened his eyes.
He shivered, gasses hissed, and helped his stiff torso to rise,
He walked, so dreamlike, in between the endless rows of cots,
Haze still filled his mind, and pain still tied his limbs in knots.
He joined the silent queue of naked men with heavy heart,
As one by one collected heavy armour, moved apart.
His weighed his spirit lower, and he chanced a glance behind,
Robots loaded empty cots with broken up mankind.
He stumbled into place beside another in the tank,
Passionless he looked across upon a face so blank.
Blue eyes empty, mouth so slack, depilated skin,
Sadness joined the emptiness that ate away within.

As silent engines tugged the tank from brightness into dark,
Raymar's sanity crept back, but battle left it's mark,
Each time he fell, each new regeneration, took its toll,
Machines could mend his body, but they couldn't heal his soul.

Michael Adams

EDDYSTONES LIGHT

Beacon tall, so steadfast
Shining in the night,
Rays of hope - a warning
Mariners all heed their plight.

Oceans roar now crashing
Hells-teeth, the sirens drone
Nature's cruel might - unbeaten
A watery grave, far from home.

Winds and rain about us - our
Canvas in tatters now
Faint hearts, exhausted bodies
Too much for us - but how

Shall on these rocks we leave her
Should fate decide the rest,
Come on my lads, pull together
And show the devil who's best.

Hearts of oak - recovered, 'til
All the heavin's through,
At last we're making headway
We're clear, me bullies - true!

Thank God for old 'stones light
Many lives were saved this day,
Now homeward bound, me hearties
Trim sail, for Whitsand Bay.

Michele Williams

HER TIRED EYES

Beneath her tired eyes I see,
What she must once have seen of me,
Now her eyes look upon,
A loveless life that once shone.

And in her arms once filled with need,
The glowing warmth from which I did feed,
There was so much for me at stake,
The love on which I grew was fake.

And deep within her own heartbeat,
The pounding rhythm once so sweet,
All she gave me were the skies!
The clouds I rested on were lies.

And from her lips I hear,
The sounds which I could once hold dear,
She only made my life worthwhile,
Now my life's not worth her smile.

And in her own mind I know,
the mindless thoughts are still in flow,
I had so much love to share,
Now she has no time to spare.

And in her soft touch I feel,
feelings which were once so real,
They gave an inner warmth and heat,
She's gone and I am incomplete.

Dan Griffiths

READING

When I read Dickens, I was cast
As Copperfield and feckless Pip;
Young, ambitious, yearning, loving,
Growing up in passion's grip.

When I read Shakespeare rather later,
I *was* Hamlet, doomed, alone,
Moody, brooding, angry, drifting,
Paring meaning to the bone.

When I reached my mid-life crisis,
Chaucer lent me style and wit;
Wise, ironic, broad, sardonic,
Human nature's counterfeit.

When I reached my final dotage,
I could sympathise with Lear;
Awkward, powerless and erratic,
Wishing I could see and hear.

So my life's last act approaches,
But, because I'm not quite dead,
Though I'm Lear, I'm also Hamlet,
Pip, and all the rest unread.

Andrew Bent

ANYONE OUT THERE

Speaking to you from the words on this page
A person whose heart is filled with rage

These feelings follow me throughout the day
Yet I'm still not sure what to say

It's like there's no one listening out there
And if there is I'm not so sure they care

And this fleeting moment that I speak to you
is a moment that is a moment too few

For soon you'll forget what was said
And finally when I'm past and gone

I will never know if I ever did convey
The horror and injustice I feel each day

James A Gardiner

ELGAR

No words describe the soaring
            painful ecstasy of strings
the secret self has wings
While salt rivers course down
            life mapped cheeks
warm sweet winds caressing
            golden hills
whispering the nearness of pure joy.
Across the minds sound painted
            canvas a figure dances
perfection, unhindered, free.
If music made by man
            can lure the senses
            to the brink - just think
What lies beyond for you - for me?

Betty Norris

COMMUNION

She's there most days -
seated on a mound above dilapidated roundabouts,
shuttered tea and coffee stalls, a line or two of washing,
the unchained dog rampaging in the drizzle.

She doesn't opt for picturesque surroundings -
most likely couldn't pull her shopping trolley further
or wants to know she's not too far from habitation
as, alone and mildly trembling, she feeds the birds.

They settle round her, peck across her shoulder,
treat her like a latter-day St Francis -
their wariness of other humans undiminished
by their trust in her -

if any come too near or loud they scatter,
chorus over caravans and puddles,
chagrined as she is to have their feast disturbed:
the giving and receiving of the bread.

Virginia Rounding

THE ROBIN

No longer he'll come with winter snow,
to hop and fly beneath the thorn hedgerow,
Now cold and still, breast of faded red,
a pile of leaves for his death bed.

R N Irwin

SOCIETY TALK - BETWEEN THE WARS

She didn't dear -
Did you hear -
My God, Oh no -
What! - let her go -

And what is more -
Not on the floor!

No more I pray -
Tho' perhaps you may
She's hardly one of us -

I took -
Don't look
She's coming over -
She must be older -
My God -
That's odd!

Hello, dear -
Do sit here -
You look pale -
In the sale!
Oh! a too, too fright-
Not twice in the night!
Oh! a shame -
I'd blame
Your dressmaker if I were you -
Oh! you do!

Well - come to tea -
Now let me see -
Yes, fine -
At nine -
Bye, bye dear - see you at -
Darling - who the hell was that?

Peter Wait

JUST ANOTHER LIFE

Another child's dream
And another fading spell.
Another dying man
Living in his hell.
Another misplaced childhood.
Another broken soul.
Just another life
That failed to reach its goal.
Another shooting star
Burned out before its time.
Another teenage child
Trapped in a life of crime.
Another single mother
In one room with her charge.
Another bloody murderer
Who is still at large.
Another business man
Cheating on his wife.
At the end of the day
It's just another life.

Lee Swallow

THE MISTRESS

The rush of the hull
The slap of the sails
Up to the mark
And round the buoy
The final run with a following tide
And back to port for pints of joy.

Some tricks seem short
And some seem long
Each different in a subtle way
Seducing sailors back to the sea
Is it idyll or battle in store today?

Don't ask me why I sail the sea
There is no answer I can give
God put it there with its deaths and joys
And I'll live for it whilst I shall live.

J W Anstice Brown

SINE NOMINE

'I believe in equality,' said Stalin
Sitting in an ornate chair
Overlooking poverty.
'And this I have achieved.'

'As do I,' said Hitler
Knocking back an agreeing Jew.
'But only in my people.'

And the sun went down
And the sun came up
And in time the world won over.

For if the top of the tower
Is down on the ground
Why bother climbing the stairs?

Lucinda Peckett

GLENFINNAN

As you stand at the head of the glen
With the monument by your side.
you can hear the tramp of hundreds of men,
Come to serve their Prince with pride.

As you stand at the head of the glen,
Your thoughts may wander free,
Think of the hope in the breasts of them
And the Prince who came from the sea.

The standard was raised at the head of the glen,
The clans vowed to fight and strive,
Imagine the surge in the hearts of men,
For the Prince and the *forty five,*

As I stand at the head of the glen,
The memory lingers on,
Of heroic deeds of those highland men,
And of the Prince who is gone.

And now all alone at the head of the glen,
Stands a highlander built of stone,
As if awaiting the call again,
For the Prince to claim his own.

Ian Muir Martin

THEM

In the end it seems a convincing form of survival
to those who remain, they having left behind
the often amazing things by which we remember them,
huge jokes, perhaps, potable bottles of wine,
an innings of five hours for sixteen runs,
a way of being always the same. Ourselves.

We hang around, wishing we could see them,
aching to hear their latest smart remark,
address a dish that only they could cook,
delight in their inimitable account
of some impossible mix-up in Samoa,
coming to wonder whether there has been
an ebbing away or a flowing in.

We too long to be treasured, at least not forgotten,
and it is inconceivable that none of us will be here
or, worse, that you will be the last.
It's happening to someone now, just as we speak.

Peter Bostock

WANTING

'I would do whatever you wanted me to do.'
And you who always claimed you were too proud!
I push the promise back across the pillow, saying: likewise
I for you.
Knowing that while I will want aloud,
Your wanting will stay shuttered up behind those clear blue eyes.

Carrie Blackford

COMING HOME

Bus home, I get on. Busy today, hardly a seat.
Find a space although it's a tight squeeze.
Shopping - on knees or on floor?
Decide on floor, looks more casual.

Bus jolts off, bumpy ride but no-one minds
Quite jolly, finished work. Friday Afternoon.
Smile at big woman in seat opposite.
Man next to me seems nervous
looking distractedly out of the window
he tries to ignore all the women.
So many women.

Bus jolts, shopping bags tumble, better keep hold.
Bus getting fuller and noisier, lots of laughter.
A voice from the front of the bus asks
'Is this anyone's potato?'
'It's mine' I blush.

Runaway potato is passed back, hand by hand, over the heads
I thank them.
Return my dinner to its bag and beam at my travelling companions.
Happy people smile back.
It's Friday Afternoon.

CW

A LONG TIME DEAD

You're a long time
dead.
A long time
searching,
for those words said
in drunken babblings.
A long time
wishing,
for yesterday's dreams.

You're a long time
dead.
Smashing your head,
against brick walls.
Sorting out the laughter,
from the screams.
A long time
learning,
how to stay alive
in this jungle.

You're a long time
dead.
Sleeping,
in someone else's head.
Waiting,
for them
to crawl
out of bed.

K J Furnival

24

SCENE FROM BRIDGE

Upstream, sun catches showering jets
Which froth out white below the dam.
But here, slow-moving Guinness water;
Steep banks staved with wooden fencing -
The waist-high nettles falling anyway -
And a shrub, arms reaching over: sinking.

Beyond the dam: dark mirror surface;
Stippled lightly by dancing midges,
And a blackbird, gently kissing as she passes.
Butterflies - flickering over nettle clumps -
Glimpse their reflections in the stillness. And in love
Drift down but, sensing jeopardy, spin free from thrall.

All around dense green overpowers,
The sun beating down from a cloudless sky.
Except under leaves, where shadows lie -
Defining each tree's separateness.
In the long grass, two figures, face to face,
A small child's head, jutting from a back.

Three dogs sniff erratically along the bank,
And a brown bird rises, falls, across the meadow.
In the blue, a spot of white becomes a streak.
An aeroplane's low hum carries to the bridge -
Reminder of the world of transport where
Cars pass, tyres purring, a train rattles over rails.

F M Bradley

IMPRISONED WITHIN THE BALLROOM OF MY MIND

Dance with me now lonely lover,
Let's waltz to the lone violin.
Move with me now lonely lover
Dance that my heartstrings shall ring.

Dance in my bitter sweet tear,
Imprisoned in a watery eye.
The vision of my lone ballerina
All etched in the tears that I cry.

Swirling across the hall slowly,
Away from my two empty arms,
Weaving a spell of seduction
As you leave with your passion and charms.

Please dance with me now lonely lover
To the strain of my lone violin,
encased in the light of my crystal
To end where my life should begin.

Now I gaze at you dressed in black satin
Swirling around in the mist,
Flaunting yourself and your partner,
My jewel, my lost amethyst.

Yes, look at the man you left naked,
so naked and devoid of love.
A man that can look from a distance,
A stranger, a prisoner of love.

I F Grey

WE CAN'T ALL PLAY THE LEAD IN SNOW WHITE

Notice me!
I am crying out to be noticed.
Silly, vain, stupid person that I am,
I want, I need, I crave,
Love and affection, to belong!
I too; would like to be special.
Do I have to wait until the half hour of my funeral
To have my Eden time.
It is only my body that is twisted,
If you can spare the time to look deep into my eyes,
You will find that my soul can run, dance, and laugh with you.
I have opened my door and thrown out my embarrassment,
So if you can do the same,
Please! Please! do knock and enter;
The warmest of welcomes awaits you.

June Plaskett

RED

Red of blood and red of fire,
Red of life and red of death,
Man lays waste,

Red of sky and red of earth,
Red of wounds and red of fur,
Man lays waste.

Red of bark, red of spark,
Red of sap and red of meat,
Man lays waste.

Red of dust and red of sky,
Red of fire and red decay,
Man lies wasted.

A M Swandale

REMEMBER YOU

I walked past your house today
barren trees naked in frost
the last apologies of leaves
now brown and skeletal in form
dance closer to their gutter death.
The summer air once so soft
now bites and stings with every breath
a constant reminder of the bitterness.

Unbending branches snap with sorrow
under feet that have no feeling
inside your house it's colder
now, than it is outside
landscape bleaker from the inside out
the promise of warmth in pieces
hopes lie scattered amongst dead flowers.

The summer has been laid to rest
an epitaph engraved in ice
a resurrection miracle cannot be
the tears are shed, wreaths have withered
longing will not recreate the past
'they loved those who loved not them'
these words preserved in ice
will melt away come spring.

Diana Mitchell

JANUARY FIRST

We were wording, talking, thinking:
wading down the sludge of feelings
exhausted through their old repeatings
deep within our lives' grey walls,
hoping to catch a fractional gleam
in our fusty straw-damp stalls

>   Until we stepped clean
>   out upon the moors
>   spoke within the solemn
>   winter-fingered trees
>   and strode the tawny grasses
>   to the circled secrecy
>   of the ancient stones

>   The sun beamed
>   its meridian majesty
>   through our bound frames,
>   igniting the subtle flames
>   of our spiritual wings
>   spreading out wide to greet
>   the sky's sweet horizon
>   singing a simple diapason
>   open and clear
>   for the birth of the new year.

Adam Meya

A MEASURE OF LOVE

Each time they meet he puts the child to test.
'How much do you love your mother now?'
Young arms like sapling branches stretch.
Wider and wider. Tender muscles strain.
Eyes, ardent with the thought of love,
Only half see the kind-old-uncle face.
'That brother, too, show me how much you love him.'
A smile; arms stretch an inch or two less wide.
'Your sister?' And he takes her down the list
Of friends and playmates, relative and pets
While silently she tells her love for each
With hands flung out or almost palm to palm.

The child's integrity is uncorrupted yet
By manners, gratitude or thought of gain . .
He keeps the light of laughter in his eyes,
Hiding absurd anxiety, as he asks
The final 'How much do you love -?'
Suppose the little hands should fling less wide
Than when they last played out this game!
Or dare he hope they'll show a bigger span?
But no, the measure's very near the same.
He laughs, half rueful, half relieved,
Glad to be loved, though still three inches less
Than that old mongrel dog!

Freda Hurt

30

DAPHNE

Sunseekers all
Learn from me:
I was the one
Sought by the sun -
Which is new.

Some people run
Faster than others
Whether chased or not.
I got caught.

And from then on
It was a question
Of morals
Or laurels.

Poems are made
By fools like you
About me.
Or would you rather be
A tree?

Terence M Cluderay

PASTORAL

I heard a man who called the cattle home;
He leant upon a mossy five-barred gate.
His face was weather-burnt, and seamed as earth,
His clothing greyish, of uncertain date.
Patient he stood, as Pan himself might stand,
And now and then he sent his desolate cry
Across the hill, until I almost thought
To see the country gods haste in reply:
And here indeed they came, soft-breathing, slow,
Pressing the daisies with their solemn tread.
Stately and grave, broad sides sun-warmed and sleek,
Crowned with fierce-curving horns each gentle head.
Across the lambent haze of afternoon
The ancient call caressed the silken air,
Mingling with echoes in the dreaming hills
Where once his fathers' voices sounded there.
Beyond the gate the brazen modern world
Swept past unceasing with the shriek of speed:
His eyes gazed only on his timeless field;
Patient he stood and called, and paid no heed.

Audrey Hughes

THE REMEMBERING

And in the remembering
I think I hear a voice whispering
a distant sound yet distinct
that permeates all around
it keeps calling me imploring me
to just follow my own instinct
telling me that I have a choice
to carry on in the same tired way
or answering unto You I pray
that You refresh me be my deliverer

And in the love that generates
I'm still left wondering . . .
what do you who do you belong to?
But then I realise I recognise I remember
the Voice within is the Voice without
there can be no doubt - You are me and I am You

And I'm smiling now remembering . . .

Fiona Jo Clark

KNIGHT FIGHTER

In battle armour about your quest,
Swarming skies, fields of arrest,
With stalwart defiance fought by the few,
In air of conflict, seas of blue,
For deeds and daring have no regret,
Knight of the sky, lest we forget.

Susan Priestley

COVERING

There they all were -
young; not so young,
old, not so old,
and I.
Human gathering-instinct,
life-long frenetically
covering the hole left
remaining.
Pulling the strings together
tight
or as tight as the frightened
small ones can.
Funeral past.
Sighs of relief or of something.
I the eagle,
wings outspanned to cover
'neath the true covering
the broken, tired ones
for pity's sake.
There they all were -
young, not so young,
old, not so old,
and I
a million years old

Annie Glass

34

SHE WAITS FOR HER ELECTRIC STOVE

She waits for her electric stove
to ignite the cigarette
that kisses its ever-decreasing
spiral hob.

A dying, yellow sun
illuminates the iron-framed window
supplying her with a large,
rectangular halo.

A beautifully rounded silhouette
she slouches, hand-in-pocket,
like
John Wayne.

Gary McKie

SO SAD TO GO

So sad to go, but could not stay.
Just made it to your tenth birthday.
The car did not slow down a jot.
Afterwards did not even stop,
Only left you laying in the road.

The judge in court, said you must be jailed.
For the way, that you had behaved.
And a guilty conscience, you will keep.
Forever in you somewhere deep.

Your drinking and driving, killed my son.
And he was my only one,
I only hope, when you have kids.
You never have to go through this.

K Hullah

CLEARANCE SALE

In an Auctioneer's hall, what was obviously a complete home was on offer.

No bidders for the sideboard
  Of plywood oak veneer,
On which the hard-earned luxuries
  Confirmed the festive time of year.

No takers for the table
  With polish enhanced grain,
Except where drink spilled years before
  Became a much regretted stain.

This, where the family gathered
  And meals were served with pride,
Had watched the infant in high-chair
  Bring home for tea his future bride.

Someone did take the vases,
  A few pans from the stove.
The trinket brought by friend who'd been
  On Summer holiday in Hove.

The bedroom clock was offered,
  And was, like most things cheap.
For something that was wound each night
  To tick through fifty years of sleep.

The Auctioneer reminded
  That he was there to sell,
So took a bid that bought the lot,
  And then the final gavel fell.

And so the home of fifty years,
  A married lifetime's span
Now faces times that are unclear,
  Piled in the brown-smocked dealer's van.

John Arbee

NORMAN DREAMING

There are only four screws which bind his bed.
But the iron rivets under the bed-boards
brace themselves for another long night.
In Sleep's limbo his bulky weight is cast adrift
In a universe so dry, his dreams are small and intestinal
Not really dreams at all
but facsimiles of faded shades and passions.
Histories of a childhood he could not bear
Lusts he now derides in crowded tap-rooms.
In saliva dribbles and sonorous bursts
Like a bilge pump he cranks up, half rises and rolls
Flattening out the creases in his sheets.
His dog sleeps uneasy below his bed
Strangled in bouts of hollow barking.
No night shadows or moons haunt this room
The double-lined polyester curtains see to that.
When he awakes at dawn; he will scratch and yawn.
Yell at his dog and walk a field or two.
In sleep as in wake his dreams are similarly met.
He will eat his weight and kill a bird or two in sport.
He'll hear the bellow of a cow
But not the bluetits in the hedge.
In this primeval path he finds his succour.
Only fools and kings have deep dreams - that's for sure
In the late afternoon's eddy, he yawns.

Jane Park

AMMONITE

I bought a shiny ammonite
In a fossil shop.
I thought that it would not be right
To take a pick and chop
Into the cliff
Wondering if
I'd harvest a good crop.

And so I chose this polished shell,
Long changed into a stone,
Preserved so that the rocks can tell
Of wonders they have known.
Their mystery
Saved up for me,
Now beautifully shown.

Its glossy spiral neatly curled
Looks more like jewellery
Than something from the living world,
A creature of the sea.
Though saved with care,
Not really there,
A well kept memory.

The simple segments join and turn
To make the pattern fine,
As in the furling fronds of ferns,
A spiral by design.
Three-d photo
Of long ago,
This ammonite of mine.

Susan Perks

MIND GAMES

Void of emotion,
Detached from the world,
Thinking of nothing.
Then it comes,
That minuscule thought.
An innocent creature,
or so it appears.
That minuscule thought,
See how it grows.
Turning darkness into light,
Black light.
Now there are many.
Thunderous beasts,
Invading your mind
And tormenting your soul.
Its will is too strong,
Eroding your sanity,
Then it is gone.
Gone but not forgotten,
You carry its scar.
that minuscule thought,
That innocent creature.

A Wilson

CHRISTMAS

Christmas has gone now,
>With its trees and its lights.
The mountains of food and,
>Its wines, reds and whites.

The oranges and apples,
>The chocolates and nuts.
The 'fridge packed so tightly,
>Its door wouldn't shut.

And midst all this goodness,
>No one gave a thought.
For the ones that are starving,
>Their plight means just naught.

Old men and young ones,
>Imprisoned on some lie.
Small children are shot,
>By some fool, tell me why?

The fires and deep flooding,
>Perhaps earthquakes too.
Making them homeless,
>It's not just a few.

So Christmas has gone now,
>So happy for some,
But for many only hope,
>That a quick death would come.

A B Hughes

THE SCALES OF LIFE

Strings of rhythm,
Rhythm of chord,
Cord of embryo,
Chain of man.

A slave,
To a serpent,
A saint to a God.

And all they say,
Is,
Serve me.

A till with a queue,
And when the money's made,
You're paid.

And then you're weighed,
On the scales of life.

Sandra J Middleton

REGRET

With regret, I see I cannot leave,
The thought of you behind.
I'm strong enough to walk away,
But, you're constant close to mind.

If only things didn't weigh;
So heavy on my heart.
I'd find a way to try to stay,
And act my rightful part!

S Ashby

TRI-HARD TO SUCCEED

Cold, wet and breathless,
Coming in from the swim.
Surely no fun,
In a run,
With a cycle to fit in?

What's the point?
What fuels the fire?
Is competition,
Their burning desire?

The anguish, suffering and pain.
What to gain?
Self achievement for some,
For others fortune and fame.

It takes grit, determination,
Commitment too,
To be in contention,
Not to mention,
The training you must do.

Sports people from all ages,
Somehow complete the three stages,
Showing true spirit,
When, at the end of the race,
Even the prizeless,
Have a smile on their face.

T B Stanley

THE RETURN

She loved the rose of her soul.
And milked kindness.
Her dreamscape eyes wandered
Their own warming focus
Upon books and objects that
Had once been dear,
To us.

I
Do not know
How time took her.
I
Know
We walked through secret fields of our own formation.
That was a place for moments,
When even Beethoven was dirge.
But lost space of mutual creation
Can never be recalled.

I had known her.
Then
All I saw was presence:
I was glad when she left.

John Durrel

US AND THEM

A well tended garden from devoted one,
A song or a poem, spoke or sung,
A vision of heaven promised to all,
Success or failure, rise or fall.

Happy, excited aimless and free,
Looking, expecting, demanding to succeed,
This aim of mankind selfishly thought,
With disregard of feelings of any sort.

With many the futures shadowed with fears,
Of imminent earthquakes, or raging floods,
And some can only see the spilling of blood,
Whilst plenty more don't give a damn,
They play their part, even if it's a sham.

Others kindly help to ease,
Burdens of others, sometimes diseased,
Some give their lives, that others might live,
There's many thousands out there wanting to give.

So even though plenty despair,
Let them take notice that many do care,
To help and assist as best they can,
To live one's life whatever the span.

Charles Long

AN INNOCENCE LOST

Love is like a soft spring breeze
That blows so gently through the leaves
But the love of a child is so much more
So forgiving and kind, gentle and pure.
The love of a child asks for nothing
Except for you to fill the yearning
To learn and experience everything new
And also hoping to receive love from you.
A child's innocence is so rare
In these days of fighting and war
All they see is greed and hate
For the loving side of people they must wait
But for how much longer will they grow
If fighting and war is all they know
It's time to turn this world around
And teach the children where love can be found.
It is deep inside us everyone
Just waiting for us to find
But how, I hear the voices crying out
Just give your child a hug and you will see
That the love and innocence of a child
Is in every one of us
Just look deep into a child's eyes
To see the pain when they cry
A child's life should be full of fun
Not spending each day playing with a gun.
Mankind sees the wars as a necessary measure
But from the pain who can gain pleasure?
A child's love and innocence is such a joy to see
But in this harsh and cruel world it is a rare commodity
Let us look into our children's hearts to see what must be done
To cease this careless fighting and live again as one.

Kate Carbino

A DUEL IN THE SKY

Earth stands fearless
As menacing clouds
In anger descend
Wearing dark shrouds

A raging storm breaks
Lightning strikes sky
Then in disdain
Clouds burst rain.

Thunder rends air
In a war-like sound
Detonating echoes
Of a battleground

Warfare erupts
A duel in the sky
Elements clash
In a battlecry.

All is calm now
Sun beams through
Earth refreshed
Reborn anew

Then high above
Does nature apply
A rainbow of peace
A jewel - in the sky.

M Docherty

BULLY

Life can get you down, tackling your problems you sort them out.
Not everything is so simple, things can make you sad.
I should know I've been through it suffering in silence.
Not having many friends I didn't have anyone to turn to.
As I got older I found life at home didn't help.
Tempers flowed becoming frightening when arguments erupted.
Times when you need a friend, when you're all alone afraid of violence.
Feeling nervous and tension around my Father.

The days became unbearable I ran away twice.
Both times as a result of rows, I was too upset.
A third time and I'll never come back ever again.
It's a wonder how I haven't gone already.
At night I couldn't sleep tears were in my eyes.
These are the days that you can never forget.
Being shy and quiet it's never easy to open up to anyone.
It takes someone special, someone understanding who's willing to help me.

Bringing back memories of three bullies at school
who continuously picked on me and a friend.
Only I thought of a cunning plan to stop them
leaving a note to a teacher they were soon dealt with without them
knowing a thing.
As things were getting to me at home along came a visitor, Jim
my Uncle.
Travelling from Scotland who came to stay, I knew I couldn't pretend.
We were sitting on our own in the room
feeling emotional and under strain I actually told him.

Remembering my childhood days I recall my fear.
The times my Father went out drinking only to come back drunk.
I heard the arguments and still recall the beatings whilst upstairs.
Me I'm too gentle, I wouldn't hurt a lady I'd treat her with respect
and now I face it when he just can't control his temper, it happened
so regularly.

Being so depressed, fed up in life maybe I'll stand on a bridge and jump.
I dream of a beautiful girl to come along who cares.
The world can be cruel, animals are slaughtered, people go to war full
of hatred.

Edward G Scullion

ANOTHER FIVE SETTER

Stretching, warming, brain thinking,
Hitting gauging, game starting,
Heart rate rising, slowing moving,
Timing out, steadily losing.

No control, always running,
Receiving end of endless cunning.
Change of plan, game too light,
Now no option, time to fight.

Changing gear, up the pace,
Watch expression on the face,
Apply the pressure, make it hurt,
Clammy feel of sweating shirt.

Hour gone, brain in code,
Body ready to explode.
Time to test the power of will
Moving in for final kill.

Match point winner, turn to shake,
Slight relief from total ache,
Is this why we work and strive?
Almost dead, yet so alive!

Denis Secher

CAROUSEL

A ruined castle
By a river
Watching seagulls fly
I am a rock
Come from the isle
Somewhere 'twixt sea and sky
Coloured blue or
Coloured green
Flecked with white tops glowing
White clouds fly
Wind blows with sigh
Sun burns when it's showing
Where are you;
Wondering if or whether?
Going up or coming down
Will my time be ever?

Some are old,
Summer new
Winter comes in Season
Start in time
End comes soon.
Living without reason.

Dennis Studd

NATURE SO WONDERFUL

'Isn't Nature wonderful'
I think my friends are crazy
as they witter at a sunset
or peer into a daisy
with a fatuous expression
that indicates decay
or wilting mental acumen
as once again they say
'oh isn't nature wonderful
just look at all these bees.
The way they make that honey . . .'

These bees are on their knees!
They're sick of flippin' honey
but what else can they do?
Training schemes and jobs for insects
are remarkably few.
And what about the little lambs
that gambol in the meadow?
Nature's snake-eye dice are loaded
those cuties soon are deado.

Cobwebs frosted sugar spun
glistening with dew
a fairyland of gossamer . . .
well, just let me tell you
that weeny macho spider
climbing up the web
with his weeny box of Milk Tray
is on his last leg.
She's waiting, she's bigger
she's bolder but thinner
and after he's wooed her -
she'll have him for dinner.

Sylvie Farquhar

TEMPTATION

40 years/40 days, either way this stay feels like forever:
the searing desert's endless, toast-dry toast-brown;
sun blinks off/on off/on but otherwise that sky's changeless
unless obscured by sandstorm. And here comes one.
Nope, it's a salesman - and what a pitch: 'Y'wanna *own* all this?'
Resistible. 'Get thee behind me,' you reply (archaic for 'flake off')
and go back to building castles in the air. Might be cool there.

Given hopes of heaven springing from an in-your-face vision of hell,
suppose he appeared as the Ice King, bringing brochures on Meribel?
Not a hard sell. Neither is Zell.
Say he offered Zurs, could you demur? Who'd pass on Snowmass?
Profess you'd sneeze at Chamonix? Oh, please!
You'd drool when Satan cooed 'values galore, even cheaper in Italy!'
Maybe just half a soul - heck, who needs more?

And what if he threw in a preview? The best tempters do
so let's suppose our devilish dervish starts to whirl?
Say sandgrains and ice and brighten, the dunes grow tall and whiten
then he calls in some trees - well, you know wood, you'd get ideas.
Ready/go, you hit the snow. Now clouds blow over
- revealing grades of light and altering actual textures.
You halt on edge as Nature speaks on cue: 'This holy enough for you?'

Toward the world unfurled at its positive best for seduction
you glide faster. 'Watch your ass, Dear,' Nature insists
and conditions reshift. You tumble. Earth rumbles: 'See here.
I'm a fabulous lover, not your mother. I expect close attention.'
As you sputter through laughter - 'Maybe next year Jerusalem,
more likely year-after' - you sight a higher peak and hear: 'Whenever.
No hurry. And now you know how to look, watch for trick shrubbery.

'When Moses climbed, you figure he got only stone letters?
Kid, life can be worse but it doesn't get any better!'

Katherine Harris

IN THE HOSPICE

Hands, O be gentle!
For you are young and very strong,
And life unshackled flows along
Those tapering fingers that so thoughtless brush
My tired face, that can so quickly crush
My little flame with one swift, careless touch.
You do not even realise your own power;
You have not time, as I have, hour by hour
As each day forges new links in my chain
Of wasted opportunities and pain,
To watch yourselves. You are the wind
That blows my body clean, and brings new birth
To my stagnating flesh. To me you are
As needful as the Wise Men's star
For guidance. You are water in a land
Of heat and raging thirst - these hands I dread
That spin my life out on its tenuous thread.
I hate - because I need them; and you could
So quickly hurt and mangle if you would . . .
I wonder - I your living parasite!
You are so strong, and yet your touch so light.

Margaret Seccombe

HILDA PARNELL

What are you
Stripped and shivery starveling?
Thing of oak, of yawning ribs.
Stocks mouldering,
Stapled in iron rusting.
Relic of quiet decay
When the river fell.

What were you?
Blackened, forgotten memorial
To secret mistress,
Slipping in and out of lover's moonlight dreamings.
Or in marauding fancy
Viking ship
On the bend of the river
In the mist of celtic time.

Abandoned dream,
Bite of dry timber,
Broken,
In and out of time.

Michael J Breen

THE HUNTED

I can see them now;
Scarlet coats billowing in the wind.
The sight I dread,
These people whose lives are full of sin.
The horses stamp their feet
They wait, impatient, for the Hunt to start,
Then the worst sight of all;
The baying hounds run, in and out they dart.

Now I must run,
I must escape this one while I can,
Before they come, fast
Horses and hounds, woman and man.

I remember once before, when I was nearly caught.
I remember the terror when I knew it was me they sought.

The forest was my saviour then;
If it had not been there, I would be dead.
I ran through the undergrowth
As thoughts rushed through my head.
The hounds got trapped,
They could not follow me through the thick bush
But I thought they would get me,
I only just got out, at a push.

So now I'm thankful
As I watch this new Hunt, that I am alive.
For sure today
Another fox will be hunted and could die.
Now I should go
Back to the Earth where I was born
But wait, what's that?
It is that dreaded sound, the Huntsman's horn.

Melanie Bullivant (16)

THE SILENT OCEAN

A sound seeking refuge; a cry for compassion?
An echo bleeding into silence.
And the ripples die on the surface.

Scarred; am I of this kind?
Stained; do the tears fall
Seared; in a conscious mind.

The figures blur in frenzied pursuit
To appease a rapacious desire
To suffocate the scream to a murmur
Replace the beauty and perfection
With a memory.

These images we have seen
It is not delusion or fallacy
It is a savage reflection
That finds its home in so many

A voice from the bowels of depravity.

Stained, the tears fall
Scarred; am I of this kind?
Paralysed, by futility.

G Morgan

LEAVES

Autumn brought us to the ground,
You and I colourfully lying,
Waiting for the mud to move around
And bury us in the winter-clay.

Hey Leaf! Do you remember
That darksome night last summer
When the wind got up from the West
And I saw my family parted from the branch,
One by one succumbing to the blast,
Myself failing almost at the last?

And other things remembered.
Can you not still feel that dying bee
Weakly clinging to your veiny shell
That I was able, tenderly
With the breeze's aid
To move from thee?

And what of Summer-heat
When blossoms headily subdued
Us all so that we slept through perfumed hours,
Neither moving nor sensing
Anything but light and shade?

Well here is Winter now
As foretold to us when we were young
And like the many generations before us gone,
(As many as the years of man),
So shall we fade and feed
The myriad flowers and leaves to come.

William Binns

NEVER . . . TOO LATE

Never gave him a hug - when I should have

Never said thanks - for mowing the lawn, mending the car,
     going shopping in town

Never cared for the day he'd had, only mine - changing
     nappies, the feeding, the crying

Never told him, often enough, how much I loved him, and
     when I kissed him goodnight didn't say 'sleep tight'

Never troubled too much when I ironed his shirt and creased
     the collar, so much else to do - couldn't bother

Never cherished, as much as I could have, the flowers he
     picked from our garden, roughly placed in my hands with
     'there you are my darlin''

Never imagined the car would swerve, and mount the kerb

Never dreamed of life without him . . .

Never thought . . .

Jane A Steele

A SIGH

A sigh, a wish, a fear,

 I dream,
 I love,
 I live.

I scream, I hate.

I die.

Louise Melbourne

THE HOUSE OF PLENTY

Anxiousness glints in a young man's eye
as he sits and waits for his slice of pie.

White knuckles grip a pushchair
attached to an angry lady with the unkept hair.

Heads turn to a screen which clicks over numbers,
the endless numbers of people clutching tickets.
Tickets numbered from zero to 99 then back again,
what a way to fill in time.

Children improvise a playground
in our 'House of Plenty'
while an old man snores his bottle empty.

Behind steel panels and grilled glass sits our friendly
supplier 'Pompous Ass'
reassuring then debating and generally,
Wealth Rating!
'Shit' Five Hours in a Dole Office.

Music plays to please us plebs
tapping feet and nodding heads to the rhythm of the theme tune
from the Muppets?
Then Gonzo called '63'
that was me.
So if jobless you be
and pockets empty
pop along to the House of Plenty,

Paul Harper

THAT BOOK

Right enough,
just as you said
sand
was held there
between
the pages
almost as trapped
as the
words
but
with each
gold dust grain
that
fell from the page
a chapter
of
your summer
fell
too.
I smelt the
salt sea bed of
those
Ionian waters
touched
the air
and drank your women
tasted
their
skin.

Robert McMath

CORBY CRAGS

About these whin-grey rocks the heather spreads,
A purple carpet wherein countless bees
Hold sway on sunny, pollen-drunken days
Late on in August, bracken and the trees
Sport first flecks of gold, white spotted fields
Are replete with a hundred flocks of sheep,
And waterfalls, not strident yet, run down
To deep and shady pools where salmon leap.

Peaceful in ruined old age, a castle sleeps
Close by a viaduct, unused for years,
A church the Normans built survives, its yard
Deep in cranesbill and meadowsweet and ears
Of tawny grass; the patchwork of the land
Rolls on and out, across Northumberland.

Geoff Fenwick

BLUE RAIN

As I too inch my way through time,
I see your etched feelings on your face.

A travelling together yet separate, and
Alone in our isolation.

Knowing the love I see in those loved lines
May soon be out of sight, travelling onwards
Without me, time stops in a tear,
And I too observe the first tracks of time creeping across
My still foreign face.

Helen Sherrah-Davies

AMARANTH

Children come hither with featureless faces
born to a world of desolate places,
the barren trees no longer sway
in a world no longer with night or day;
where yellow crows dine on a field of pink
and man no longer has the time to think.

Was man insensitive or just didn't care?
Now flowers don't bloom because of the air
the rancid waters of a once-clear stream
where lovers would sit and dreamers dream;
where billious clouds would float and play
in the sharp fresh air of every new day.

Each new day a challenge would bring
with sometimes the simplest little thing,
now we sit in fields of naked trees
in the humid heat, an evasive breeze;
with dark, still waters that no longer flow
that carried our dreams to and fro,
now the drudge and dread of every hour
as we continue to search for the elusive flower.

Thomas A Downey

WALKING WITH YOU, IN MOONLIGHT

We walked slowly, hardly daring to let our feet touch the ground.
Moonlight held us as if in a spider's web
But we dare not resist lest we break free and in doing so
Break its hold and then nothing would be as it is now,
Only reality, and we didn't want that.

Moonlight simplified everything into what we knew and what was
                                                          unknown.
Stark branches were filters that from above
Traced patterns of silver lace upon black earth where nothing moved,
Nor dare not move or speak in our two-dimensional world
Where a single whisper would shatter fragile illusion.

Silence was so loud that it was a blanket about my head,
Hot on my face and so close
That my breath came back to me, and I stilled my heart,
For a single leaf falling would strike us to the ground.
We shunned the horizon, circled within it, round and round.
Our fingers reach out and we touched.

There was no need to speak as we walked between moon-petrified trees,
To speak would tear us apart
With the uncaring cold dagger-thrust of finality,
Then a tear from your eye caught the moon's messenger
And lay as a jewel upon your face which was in blackness,
But I dared not capture it, not yet,

Our fingers still touched, a touch so gentle that it hadn't happened,
But I knew it, and it lasted forever,
Then you were no longer there and the jewel upon your cheek had gone
And I wished that I had taken it and held it in my hand,
The night I walked with you, in moonlight.

James Byron-Archer

OF WORLDS, DREAMS AND SOULS

My love, I die
Think not of me
As in my present state
I lie.
but remember me to vibrancy,
Before I loose this mortal tie.

This bitter breath
Was sweeter once,
This fevered brow
Was worn unlined,
These shaking hands
Could bear no ill,
These misted eyes,
To pain were blind.

My love, I die
Yet let me live
Within your present,
There, let me lie.
Remember me as I once was,
Before I lost this mortal tie.

A W Bullen

QUESTIONS FROM A BATTERED WIFE

How many days have I spent ironing then?
Twenty? A hundred? A thousand and ten?
Half of a lifetime spent ironing for men
and then cast off, kicked under again.

How many hours have I spent washing floors?
 Millions? Trillions? Light years and more;
Suds up to me elbows, hands aching and sore,
then pushed and punched and shoved out the door.

How many breaths have I sucked from the air?
Gasping and hurting, held fast in his bed
then gritted me teeth when the birth pains screwed hard
and the end was a child; but for that I'd have fled.

How many years have I lived in despair?
Flinching and ducking and screaming inside
until in the end it was too much to bear:
so now I've escaped and I'm here. Do you care?

Dorothy Johnson

MOUSONA NON GRATA

Mus Musculus the common mouse
is not welcome in this here house,
the Missis is definitely not too keen
to sit in the room where you were seen.
I've been instructed to eliminate you,
a thing I am rather reluctant to do,
but under duress I've laid down two traps,
and fervently hope you'll avoid them, perhaps,
and take the broad hint that we want you no more,
and find that it's safer to scarper next door.

G W Eaton

NIGHTMARE

Tired horizons wrestle with the tousled sun
as day's magnanimity is obscured
by brutish blackness and
all about me the demons,
pricking consciences like guilt's venomous
sword.

Once I could abide all this. The uncertainty
of greying rooms and vacant, blank skies
of velvet nothing.
Shadows of gloved claws
molesting a landscape that flawed and lawless
cries

out in ever more aching echoes
for some remembered semblance of sanity
that was ours. But that was
before we faltered, tore
out roots to accompanying roaring
obscenities.

Now I would reel from your twilight touchings,
almost spent in a moment but not quite
devoured by daring, just not
quite obliterating my
own insecurity, but enough, say, to imply
night.

For an implication will suffice, such as those
uncomfortable naggings so offered
when as infants in curtained cells,
late for torches, quaking heart
drumming undercover, we only partly
suffered.

Gwyn Winter

SPIDER

A spider now
With eyes like jewels
And hairs so delicate you shiver
I stand
On threads of memory.

A twitch of silk
Calls me to moths
Bright wasps or beetles sternly clad
Sometimes
To vibrant butterflies.

Shall I deliver thick paralysis?
Suck juices, turn them into me?
Or let them flutter 'til decay
Leaves empty scraps
To turn through many breezes?

I have this choice.
I can do all these things.
But once they're mine
I cannot set them free.

Lucy Keeler

THE ISLAND

In a sea of obscurity
On an island of anonymity,
No trees to shelter with their shade
The sun beats down relentlessly.

Fate conveyed me to this place
So long ago I had no choice,
But fate is wont to steal away
To leave me with no other's voice.

But when a soul is left alone
Hope will be a gentle breeze,
It quells the anger and the fear
It calms the deep surrounding sea.

But tides of doubt erode this shore
With the ebbing of my years,
And while I hesitate for freedom
Fate will drown my final fears.

Andrew English

TRULY MADLY SADLY

I watch as you look away,
Holding the tears behind a dam
Of masculinity.
The final embrace,
Brief, yet tender, ends
With the cool impartiality
Of embittered love:
Can our friendship not withstand
The twins of intimacy untied,
Or must we walk away -
Strangers with darkened hearts,
Forgetting the light that was.

Sarah Phinn

AWAKENING

I get days
When I ask myself
Why I carry on
I lay there and I can't face tomorrow
I need your sweet presence
to reach inside my soul
and take away my sorrow.
How can I possibly begin
to describe my loss
The emptiness inside?
How can I find a real reason
to continue
If it weren't for your memory?

I guess it's true, time heals,
Though I'll never forget you
I can never retrieve the
missing part of me,
That's with you
Can I remember a single night
I have not laid awake
Thinking of you?
The times I thought it was a mistake
and I awoke crying?
When I outstretched my arms,
But you slipped away.

Caroline Stacey

ONE PERFECT DAY

We left Perth's fair city at around 1030,
The sky was blue, where dark clouds had been,
The mountains were white and the A9 dirty
As we drove to a dreamland called Auchendean.

We passed Pitlochry and Ben Vrackie,
Over Drumochter where eagles soar,
past Kingussie and some others
And wound our way round Aviemore.

At last our destination nearer,
Adrenalin pumped through our veins,
The past now hazy, the future clearer,
A chance to throw off southern chains.

The air so clear you could see forever,
The ice so pure, the snow so white,
The frost so crisp you could hear its crunch,
With the mercury at -17 degrees C at night.

But within the walls of this white palace,
The love that glowed none could mistake,
The warmth that emanates from real log fires,
Like a lover's kiss, you just cannot fake.

The food and wine now set before us,
Mellowed strangers till well content,
The whisky smooth, the patter smoother,
A chance to dwell on time well spent.

At last peace fell upon friendships new,
As Christmas slowly slipped away,
But mark these words, for they are true,
There is such a thing as *One Perfect Day*.

P N Hope

THE YOUNG ONES

Spines bent, but still they stand,
And craning heads softly, violent smiles,
Eyes of minds ill-used, yet understanding now.
And bearing the weight of elders,
Sack of corruption hastily loaded
Reeking through bodies too soon old.

Complacency, smooth, coats all, and knowing grins survey,
Underneath deaf screams as whiteness falls.
An effort of recollection roughly attempted,
Jaded images and little success.
And still they come, army erect, valiant in lucidity,
Robbed unawares, yet understanding now.

Elena Mannion

HOTEL DU PARC

In the blue room
No-one lives.
Even the radiator is blue,
Cold colour.
This room Madame Robert left in haste
For her father's funeral.
In 1923, a certain Auguste Roland never, in fact, arrived,
Cancelled at the last minute,
Unavoidably detained at Pau.
Once, two nuns en route to Lourdes
Almost quarrelled here about a papal decree.
The blue room is a number between 51 and 53.
Everything happens elsewhere.

S K Smith

BUILDING ROLLER COASTERS

Local pensioners from positions of shelter;
Morris Minors and promenade benches
are watching the monster rise in stages
from its concrete depths.

Men whose love for heights
was part of their chosen career
face death on a daily basis
paint massive metallic plates
each placed in a specific order
as laid down by the designer

seated behind his computer
scrutinising his latest schemes in all angled 3-D
living out his childhood construction dreams
from meccano to hell-on-wheels.

On the screen, the track curls its huge ribbed form
coiling snake-like as if charmed
a thousand feet above the ground.

Wedged in tight, in hold-fast seats
Speeding heart before you start
In the distance - the peak; a near vertical incline
then the cliff-hanger-cliff-edge drop.
Tilt, tip-up, you can't fall
                              off
though your body says you will for certain
Four G-force then weightless
Scream then stunned into silence
(Unless you're already unconscious,
in which case you've wasted the experience.)

It's only £4 to have your insides rearranged
- Prepare to meet that waffle you mistakenly ate beforehand.

Jenny Fidler

COMING AROUND AGAIN

The ancient sage looks out,
Upon the same old boring scene
Watching vignettes played out,
The way it's always been.

Always wrapped up fresh and new
To start the grind afresh
A character to round, a point to learn
All with temptations to be immeshed

There's a point in life you realise
You've done it all before
Lived this life and walked this path
But this is not the face you wore

You're the alien inside the spaceship
and the voice from in the trees
You've the philosopher stone in one hand
And a broom between your knees.

K Orbell

THE BUTTERFLY

You dazzle the eye
Test the sight
As we follow your wayward
Haphazard flight
Illusive jewel -
Until you settle
On Buddleia flower
Thistle and nettle
Wings outspread
Brimstone Yellow
Admiral Red
Summers pledge
In field and hedge.

David Howell

FROM A SCHOOLGIRL TO AN UNKNOWN SOLDIER

You thought we would forget you,
As you dropped on the battlefield.
You thought wrong.

The English roses than you went
To war to impress
Withered in grief when you did
Not return.

But when 'The Last Post's' proud
Notes ring out,
The roses of the next generations
Bloom with pride

For you.
You died with a noble heart
And the courage of a lion.

Your death and the others dying
Brought peace into the lives
Of unknown generations.

We shall not forget.
So long as the history pages keep turning,
There will always be a place
For you, in people's hearts.

Lorna Goodall

A BROKEN HOUSE

A broken house,
A homeless brother.
Who shall we blame for this war
And destruction?
A burning skyline
Once was a soft, deep blue -
Now, a fiery dragon.
Our portrait of Granny
Her face blackened with soot,
A broken house
Like a shell, crushed by the waves.
Anonymous faces search for remains
Of the destruction
Of their ramshackle home.
A broken house,
A broken heart,
A mother with a child clinging
To her dead, cold body -
A child too young to understand,
With a doll clutched to her chest,
A doll of rag.
A broken house,
A broken family.
Who shall we blame for this war
And this destruction?

Ruth Goodall

SAMUEL ... VS ... (2:30)

His bleached, manicured, . . wickered fingers . . .
. . years worn by many Last Suppers . . .
Beseech again to (What's on the box tonight?) . . cowed hears,
His eyes close with squinted hope . .
Groping, . . for just one (Save-The-Church-Roof-Fund) . . heady Miracle;
But re-opening instead, to the much vaunted . . (Sports-Complex-
                                    Collection) Debacle

Just one lingering celestial-source . . flash of light . .
Not; . . the usual restless tinkling light . . caused . . .
. . by Torn Flex . .
chinking bulb . . Gullibly! . .
Just . . a hope-in Heaven . . light . . . Unvexed! . .
Not a hope-in- Hell . .
of preaching . . Anti-Confetti . . . church rule . . .
. . while congregational sanity reach for . . .
'I'm God's Only - - - Nobody's Fool'!' . . .
They; . . true only unto themselves, . . applaud . .
and ford through Love and Hymns . . and things . . .
and exude . . a . . Wish-This-Was-Over! . . . tinge; . .
And disappear . . up their own flaws.

Meanwhile, . . He sighs, and hears his own religion . . .
Vying with time . . in an unpious human Race . . .
and faces the facts about Deep-space and Sin,
Contemplates . . the End of the beginning of faith . . .
. . and the Beginning . . of the End, . . . of Him! . . .

R McLean

DOWN IT IN ONE, SON

Tap a table, knock on wood,
Chant a Mantra if it's any good.
Play the game, be in it to win it,
Drink that full bottle of hot Glenlivet.

Don't pass me by, stay and agree
There's no better friend to have than me.
Here's some money, don't you worry,
Drink your beer in a fervent hurry.

Pick it up and slam it back down,
A To-Kill-Ya slammer'll make you frown.
Drink it up, be merry with me.
Have some fun mate, what'll it be?

Bottle for you, bottles galore,
Gulp that down, have some more.
Are you feeling fine? Excellent.
Make that alcohol an ever present.

Have one more, just for the road.
I'll carry you to your humble abode.
Here's that last Whisky I saved for you.
Feeling any better? Looking pale aren't you?

Go on, down it in one, son.

Glenn Head

THE RAINBOW

The russet stallion rears angrily to heaven,
His nostrils flare; his titian mane ablaze.
His eyes, two glistening garnets, malevolently glare.
Dramatically, powerfully, he gallops across the sky.

The orange flames flicker in frolicking fun,
Cavorting their way into line. Like lovers,
Embracing, caressing, they gasp then fall
But their warmth and ardour remain.

The sun shines and spring flowers burst forth;
Crocus, daffodil, a yellow petalled carpet.
Their blooms shine, radiating happiness.
Brightly they sit, illuminating all around.

The naive Virginia creeps into place,
Her green fingers innocently reach for the sky.
Till all that is seen is an emerald patchwork,
A virgin meadow, glistening with dew.

The royal river rolls sadly along,
Its turquoise tears slowly trickling.
The sapphire waters hide feelings so deep.
This scene awash with the blues.

Then the master steps forth with His palette.
Wishing to join in, dips his brush in the paint.
Mixing colours, this time something darker,
Like midnight, but bluer: indigo.

The final jewel is presented for viewing.
The amethyst, so vividly it shines.
The vibrant violet vibrates in the sky,
And the spectrum is complete.

Peta C C Vale

SHRINK TO FIT

Burning amber fluid
scorches my throat
as I close my eyes.
As human flesh
steeped in acid,
hisses and shrivels . . .
melts the aches
and bruises inside.

But, at dawn
out of the scarred tissue
grows a small green tree
world-weary, yet vulnerable
and confused - for all
the branches are broken . . .

Sometimes I get bewildered,
so I take another hit.
It looks easier inside the bottle
so I'll have to shrink to fit.

Alexandra Saffer

THE POSH PEDESTRIAN

Blistery Mystery
Ms Ffyona Campbell
She walked the world over
Searching for fame

But when she arrived home
Most ceremoniously
No-one could pronounce her
Oddly spelt name

Jane Barlow

QUANTUM OF SOLACE

My love and I are far apart;
I count the hours till we meet.
I keep her always in my heart
And feel its upward surging beat.
Thus closer is my lover brought
And I take solace from this thought.

Enforced the parting, such is fate;
But not forever, soon we'll kiss.
So let time's torture pass at rate,
To bring me to that hour of bliss
When tensions shall, at last, unwind;
That solace lives within my mind.

I close my eyes, I see her face,
My hands can feel her soft, warm skin
And, as our fingers interlace,
I touch the magic there within.
My loneliness it doth redeem;
And I gain solace from this dream.

When our punishment is ended,
When the gods, at last, relent,
With our minds and bodies blended,
In a measured, sweet content
Lost in wondrous adoration,
Solace has been my salvation.

Gone the distance in between;
Gone the minutes, hours, days;
Gone the sombre empty scene;
Gone the parting of our ways.
From empty time and space now freed
And solace will have served its need.

R S Griffiths

THE TRUSTEES OF BRITAIN

What's wrong with an MP making mistakes
So long as he's plenty of cunning
What's wrong with a minister being a rake
So long as you know he's just funning
A lie here or there, a sly wink or two
How on earth can that make any difference to you
You know that in politics
Nothing is quite what it seems.

You know that this country is going downhill
That the government worries and cares
That the family's important to all our MPs
As they kiss their side kicks on the stairs
That a child here and there is not serious living
Has nothing to do with their work or their giving
Single parents are heinous crimes we all know
But not for a Minister, only old Joe
So please don't make a great fuss.

How could you suggest that a loose living fool
Is not a fit person to govern or rule
Integrity, faithfulness, keeping a promise
Having a love affair cannot compromise
A person who sits in the house with authority
Private life does not concern the majority
Well of the ruling class, if not the rest
So don't expect us to resign.

Mary Howell

TWILIGHT

Attention beckoned my sight to the pane,
She threw back my elemental reflection,
A shallow outline of shadows and hollows.
The operatic moon bulges through the skin of the sky,
Surrounded by a celestial symphony of stars.
The night bites with the chill of a bow,
Stretching over the taut strings of a violin.
Uneasy shuffling of the orchard,
Tenses the muscles of the air,
And night clasps her hand tighter.

The wispy shade of a cat pads the soil,
Two emerald eyes gleam as they pizzicato the hedge.
Streetlamps cast their ochre hoops,
Wedged between thick slices of darkness,
Onto the footpath weary of walkers.
The first purple flares of dawn,
Clamber across the abyss of sky,
Shedding reality onto the twilight garden.

Jon Hardy

SUMMER'S SONG

Come with me to shades of blue,
For summer's days are long,
And by this shore shall I and you
Sing this summer's song.

For days as these shall never last,
So let us sing full hearted,
And give no thought to days gone past
Nor days that have not started.

Talitha Tallett

PERMAFROST

Frosty the faces
That pass within inches
No flicker of recognition
'Though our paths often cross

Icy the resolve
Of those determined
To offer no word of thanks
For a service rendered

Like a chill wind
An ill wind
Uncensored obscenities gust
As I walk my innocuous way

Like snow, choking fissures
In the pavements of my soul
Cruelty
Is rife here

I would like to leave
Life in the South
Is not easy

'Ah but in the North
The climate is cold!'
He said.

Christine Allonby

SHADES OF BOMBAY

The Beggar:
> Blackened sky over coconut palm
> Announce the hour of pattering calm
> Waters rise
> Gutters fill
> And nullahs rush
> In wayward spill
> A beggar's hand
> Grasps the sky
> But he gropes in vain
> For he has to die

The Orphan:
> Yesterday's child
> Without a home
> Deaf to the sound
> Of hooter and horn
> Motherless daughter
> Of expelling womb
> Preparing the day
> For tomorrow's tomb

The Traveller:
> Slow plodding oxen in a timeless land
> Walk past paddies to a village which stands
> Uneasily
> By a railway line.
> Tarpaulin shacks shaded by green plantains
> See pi dogs pick from cadavered remains.
> Bare arsed men squat in a row
> To expel their turds of filth below
> The voyeurs on the Delhi express
> Who travel uncomfortably to a place of rest.

Madeline A Coles

DEATH ON THE ROAD

The heart-searing shriek of a mother,
In a flash to realise;
She will see her darling daughter
Killed right before her eyes.

One moment a young life blossomed,
Full blooming in love and in trust;
But now they sweep up the petals,
Along with the gravel and dust.

So science has hereby created,
A dragon - who in its demand;
Can swallow up all our children,
The cream of the fairest land.

So who will invent a new method
To counter this terrible creed?
Or shall all our jewels be offered
On the altar of hurry and speed?

Peter Rouse

THE DUCK . . . OR . . . 'OH, NOT AGAIN!'

Lost in a space, in a void beyond the earthly baize,
The face lost in a stare, the eyes in painful glaze
Once more with heart ripped out, and passions run so high,
The sharp left hander gazed towards the sky,
What more of skill, and longing to succeed,
The torment, anguish, and the need
Must show itself on yet another day,
While opponents celebrate, and cart the spoils away!

Wm Paul McDermott

THE PATTERN-MAKER

We took the hard way up,
The children and I
Up Blakeney Mound.
We loved the challenge which proved
Our goat-like capabilities.
We won't slip down the slippery slope! (Jane did later)

We were cut by the wind
But no one complained.
Imitation Blakeney smugglers
Strong and brave - but not so silent.
How can twenty children be silent?
Even so - natural silence there
Was stronger than voices.

Mirror puddles dabbled along the path
Creating careless patterns full of grace.
Random patterns, yet speaking of intentions.
Only they could be there, at the time, in that place.
Making a magic lane of water
Leading to a greater sea.

Standing in the sudden silence
Along by Blakeney's mud shod shore
We ourselves create the moment's pattern.
We seem related, just for now,
To each other and to the Pattern-Maker who welds
Sky, mud, laughing kids and poetry
Together against a backcloth of a winter's sky.

Shirley Valentine Jones

THE FANTASY

It was her fantasy
To be his slave;
To exist solely to do his bidding;
To be taken up, thrown aside, loved,
Hurt, kissed, ignored,
As the whim took him.

She would love him as he held her;
Long for him as she waited
Through his infidelity;
He could kill her
And if this were his wish
She would be glad.

This was the fantasy.

To how many is it granted
That their dreams should come true?

Hers did.

But the sharp whiteness of reality
Casts terrible black shadows
And her tears run fast
And unachieving
In the still loneliness
Of her dream come true.

Iris Green

HOME

To you I have returned again
Mourning yet that sad day in your way
When demolition through rolling smoke
Sang Now's the hour
while we like romanies swayed with our tack
Vowing not to fret - we will be back -

That day moriah's wind blew fast,
Wallpapers clung on half built walls,
Hailing sad good-byes, - no doubt,
Flapping like branches in tune and tune
To the rhythm of the workman's clout

Today I stroll down memory's land
Draw curtains on an empty stage,
A picture contains a spirit script.
Father of Newport we'll always recall
We are your kin, you bore us all

Here where houses like spouses cling
Smoke still reels,
I'm sealing games by young and old
where street end laughter is assessed

And chimneys with their fox's heads
Join hearth with leaded face to show
Thro' debris, as you stay, dream, sigh.

Joan Clark

FORTY ODD

I've reached the age
Where I want photographs
of family around me
When undue noise distresses me
and ailments preoccupy me
I cushion myself with comforts
and contemplate the past
and when I tell my age
please express surprise
and disbelief

You crept up
Upon that infant in your care
and mutilated her mind
with unspeakable acts
You talk and smile as usual
but a suppurating cess-head
of filth
goes on behind the mask
A day of reckoning
Comes
which even your black soul
can not envisage

Self-advocacy
The highest Court of Appeal
Appeal allowed
Thank you my lord
What is your fee?

P Cavell

SUMMERS

Remember summer gently slumbering,
When pages were read slowly,
And days were turned and
Blurred together with
Secrets.

Remember nights tent-pegged and talking,
When unheard sounds whispered scary,
And dreams were snack-filled and
Relished slowly with
Smiles.

Remember sorrows carefully cushioned,
When cuts were proudly shown,
And cures were found and
Allowed to breathe
Simply.

Remember then.

Paul Carter

ME

The least important thing
I am is me.

But that's the shape and form
which makes me be.

A holder for the
          thoughts and dreams,
A folder for the
          plans and schemes

Which make up me.

Ann Murphy

VISITING NANA

What drew me, I don't know.
We would sit facing
The fire dulling between us,
She, small and old
With eyes bright and knowing
And me, with interest and wonder
Sure of the bond
Like a strong felt tape
Worn but secure.
A natural material.

People came and went,
brightly sorting parcels of time,
But we stayed
Never troubling
Save to greet, agree or comment.

Such a strange match,
So new found and precious
And not at all fragile.

Anne Wood

THE BITTER -SWEET STATE OF THINGS

As we hold our swift embrace
and share the rhythm of our days,
I think of the bitter-sweet state of things:

of characters at odds - in love,
of silent pain soothed by
the touch that nearly cures;
of fear of loss and loss of shame,
of the hard look and the soft;
of the melody of quietude and discord of dissent,
of the bitter-sweetness of all we do and think and say.

So I plead with her who holds my life:
let not age's steady tread
bring on the coldness that can chill;
nor let the dreaded rush of hours
scar the union that is ours.

Jack Alster

THE GARDEN

Aconite so very brave
Flowering in the snow
With golden cap and mantle green
The ground takes on a golden sheen
And dimmest corners glow

With your friend the gentle snowdrop
You share the winter's cold
Little drops of clean pure white
And your cap of shining gold

You promise us that spring is nigh
And gardens soon will glow
And bulbs that slept will blossom forth
Replacing ice and frozen snow

N Gell

BENT BACK BILLY

He laughed when the children shouted, 'Bent Back Billy'
In the Yorkshire port where he had been born in 1785
In sight of Bridlington harbour - the sea his destiny.

Shake the hand of a hero
Shake the hand of a marine
Shake the hand of a veteran
Shake the hand of William Hird
Shake the hand of a man of adventure.

Frail in frame, irritable and excitable in nature
But loyal to King and country and fearless in battle.

Shake the hand of a man
Who fought alongside Nelson at Trafalgar
Shake the hand of a man
Who survived drinking the putrid waters
Of Flushing and the exported River Thames
Shake the hand of a man
Who helped set light to the White House
Before it was painted white.

Shocked when he watched six hundred men die
In just fifteen minutes off the coast of America.

Shake the hand of a man
Retired after eighteen years of loyal service
Shake the hand of a man
Whose spine was shattered by an American bullet
At the battle of New Orleans.

(Bent Back Billy now lies in an unknown grave
unsung and forgotten by history)

John Critchle

FIELDS OF BLOOD

The ghost of a woman ran aimlessly
Through the fields of blood,

And the blackness of night,
Into the whiteness of snow.

He had a hundred piercing eyes
That bore deep into her soul,

And iron fists that battered and bruised
Her tired, aching flesh.

The man she loved,
Soft as a rose, gentle as a dove,
a dreaded assassin of hope.

Her tangled web of confusion and fear,
Invisible to his eyes,

The only kisses to grace her lips,
His evil desires and lies.

She took the blows, humiliation and shame,
She'll take them to her grave,

But lurking deep in her darkened hell
Was a flickering flame of hope,

The angel of her bottomless pit,
Shone bright amid the gloom

She walked the wire to freedom,
And swore never to return.

Her courage and strength, an inspiration to others,
Her will to live, to survive,

For she that pushes the devil aside,
Deserves to stay alive.

Teresa Ducker

ONE NIGHT SKY

Contemplating weather's bruises on a battered skin,
coloured like flame treated copper and tin.
My eyes did drink in; the oil painted plateau
of gods and goddesses' ubiquitous chateau.

Indigo gases released vermilion spears.
Their edges tinged with purples.
A moon eye, blinking down on this place, peers
in through the azure; earth perpetually pulls?

Some tempest place of ideality,
the voyeur of years that proceed,
Heralded by Christianity
as the Utopia for souls disembodied.

Like a pupil, growing ever wider in the nightfall.
So immense, you could feel the universe against your skin.
If you opened your eyes tall,
you could nearly, almost, climb in.

One night sky shared with a cigarette,
never to be seen again.
A night sky, never shall I forget.
Now washed away in another day's rain.

C M Andrews

YOU WON'T HEAR FROM ME FOR A WHILE . . .

Crikey, my writing is stifled,
For once I don't know what to write,
My literary voice has a headache,
It's no longer smiley and bright.

I've got things I need to tell people,
In my own inimitable way.
When I have pens and paper and pencils,
I always have so much to say.

But my brain refuses to tick,
And my heart refuses to smile.
With an ebb in my creative flow,
You won't hear from me for a while.

Maybe I should change my audience,
Write for sad people, not those who laugh.
Maybe I should try writing elsewhere,
Like in a fish pond or in the bath.

I could shout about all the bubbles,
And the tap that goes drip, drip, drip,
Pontificate about all the lather,
And my plastic pirate ship.

I have run out of experiences to draw on,
My life is now boring and bland,
I can muster nothing from my brain cells,
Or the activities of my hand.

So now I am bereft of a voice,
Experience, imagination and style.
The death of my writing flair,
Means you won't hear from me for a while.

Jo Wright

RITES OF PASSAGE

High summer pulls the drawstring
tight around my memory;
I struggle
with bright lawns, still air,
you in your deckchair.

Autumn with its blatant shedding,
long shadows smouldering,
suits me better, cuts me loose.

I wait while slow tides bleed down
the valley like vows
of silence.

Suddenly, clearing the narrows
between barn and byre -
a volley of swifts
home in, swerving
on the wind's wires.

Grief has no meaning for them.
They return again and again
to the same place; birdskulls
catching cadences of last year's summer.

I refuse to believe that once grounded
they cannot rise.
I welcome their screams.

Ellie Owen

THE CYPRESS HEDGE

The melancholy cypress trees.
       fringe the morning sky.
The hedge is tall, tall, soaring up,
       it must be all of twenty-two feet high.

Storm-tossed foliage; turbulent movement
       up and down from side to side.
The diamond sky shines brightly
       through the chinks in the greenery wall.

Tranquil trees, foliage faintly stirring;
       sparkles of sunlight pierce the thick tapestry of green;
       the only sound the chip-chip of a morning bird.

A still, calm day of quiet misty light;
       desultory cheep or tweetle through the faintly foggy air
       as the lazy bird grooms himself, and takes his time.

Cool and still, how still the cypress trees;
       no movement, nor a breath of breeze.
The occasional chip and twitter break the stillness
       and in the valley the mist breathes quietly on.

A breeze skims through the lazy, leafy branches, then all is still;
       a quiet moment.
Then the relentless weaving and bobbing
       continues on its restless way.

Today some hope has come to me;
       I do not heed the cypress tree.
My spirits soar as bird in flight;
       let cypress mourn into the night.

Nancy Ellam

THE BLUE RIBBON

You are sitting with furrowed brow
trying to tie a bow with blue ribbon
and I love you -
- not for all you are
and all you do,
though all men praise you
(and all women envy me!);
not for your idiosyncratic wisdom
without a book to back it
nor even much reflection
yet which only seldom errs;
not because to honour and obey is,
to my surprise, my own free will
(when our ship hits hidden rocks
and I need to be reminded
that and why I love you
those may be my reasons);
- no, tonight I love you simply because
you are trying to tie a blue ribbon
round an impossibly knobbly package
for our son who will be one
and is unlikely to notice,
and you do not say, with that smile that broke a thousand hearts,
'You do it dear, you're so much better at it',
but you persevere, muttering darkly,
chewing both ends of your moustache.

Helga Dixon

SO HAPPY NOW

I don't care for Country and Western
but I sure dig The Byrds
I'm not into Charlton Heston
but I'm in love with words

I don't know what I'm supposed to know
Sometimes I feel quite fine
But I do know there's a place you can go
and Simon Says it's mine.

I'm not into Fiesta's or Astra's
but I sure love The Animals
I eat too many pastas
and I think I have mandibles!

One could say I am out of town
Temporarily indisposed
An adjective without a noun
And you'd be right, I suppose

I cruise in CV fashion
That's a Citroen type of course
When hip chicks pass with passion
we communicate in Morse

The world can't reach me here
So come on, take a bow
Celebrate with another beer
because I'm so happy now

Ash Rowell

FORGOTTEN

The track lay wide
on a beaten down day
It stretched for miles
In that forgotten way

Sitting in the middle
between two steels
On a wooden blanket
it feels so real

Birds fly by
as rabbits run
Cat chasing them
as hit by sun

Smoking a cigarette
as planes rush by
sitting in awe
wanting to cry

Drinking milk, to water mouth
Sitting alone
as if in doubt

A wonderful feeling
in such disarray
Let it be like this
my way

Gary P Foster

GENERALLY ...

I do believe it harder to control a laugh than a cry,
More cunning to conceal, a yawn than a sigh.

And most genial to seem sincere when the case is otherwise,
To be truly honest when conveying the blackest of lies.

To hide hatred with the deepest deception,
From the one to whom you show most affection.

To wear a glorified air of admiration and interest,
When polite conversation leaves you sick and depressed.

To express intelligence in all that you hear, so that none will find,
You have no acquaintance with any subject of this kind.

To pronounce understanding and sympathy,
To one who would not return such a decency.

To be true and show compassion'
Even when it is not the fashion.

To keep sorrow in a dark lonely place,
And let only joy represent your face.

To refrain from waking an evil beast,
When all reason for love and beauty has ceased.

To show indifference when the harshest wound is carved,
To be content when all of life's foods are starved.

The human being is a genius in disguise,
A miracle that lives between earth and skies.

Knows all and nothing each in turn,
Has the capacity to think, to do and learn.

Visits these places in life's journey,
To open the door you must choose the right key.

Emma Wood

LIFEWATER

Broken bones of mortal man
ground to dust and blown
to the winds.

As the dust gathers
beaches form,
from the collected sands
the bitter bones of mortal man.
Mere mortals.

In the time it takes to tell
the souls of greater beings swell
in the foam upon the shore . . .

and from the sea come waves
washed with such emotion
as from whence they came.

The fishes great and small
that feed amongst the coral
devouring the spirits that arise
                    so formed in tiny bubbles they aspire
to mingle with the foam
that washes sand
that is the bones
of mortal man.

K MacDonald

A SECRET DEFECTION

Watching her cutting sandwiches,
deftly practised, not to be disturbed,
hearing children fighting in the garden,
wondering if they should be curbed
or left to sort it out themselves,
he thinks how quickly matters harden
into this crisp efficient life,
neatly made to fit a man, a wife,
and point whatever children are the norm.
Sometimes he shuts his eyes,
escaping down a beaten track
which leads to a lost time . . .
Informal room above a busy road,
a chiming clock, a window framing skies
of every season . . . travelling back
to that high space behind his eyes
where cost and reason have no place
and something like perfection lies,
immured in his defection to the past
he says inside his head, (remembering,
above the bed, a roof-light full of clouds.)
'I come again to picture how it was . . .
The world extinguished by a kiss.
Outside, unheard, the rain spattered
and, at the corner of my eye,
a wind-scattered bird shadowed the sky.
Five struck in a corner of the room.
It was the last unfettered bliss I knew,
that warm visceral being alive in you.'

Vivienne Foster

CHAMBER MUSIC

The music comes from silence
And enters upon the stage.
The opening chord reverberates *slowly and softly*
while the melody ascends ever higher.

The incandescent aura of sound
Fills the space *slowly and softly*,
As the players remain motionless,
Poised on the brink of eternity.

The colours change *slowly and softly*
Upon the evening air.
In the distance an echo returns,
Laden with glistening gold.

A new melody gradually rises,
Tinged with haloes of blue and red.
As yet unheard in its entirety,
The music moves *slowly and softly*.

The glimmering chords process ever forward,
Touched with a shimmer of silver.
The melody moves *slowly and softly*
And reaches its ultimate peak.

The colours change *slowly and softly*
Upon the evening air.
In the distance an echo returns,
Laden with glistening gold.

The music always comes from silence,
And into silence it constantly returns.
. . . evermore *slowly and softly*.

Jeffrey Lewis

THE TREE OF MAGIC

Roots sunk deep in the ground
reach ever further down
searching, seeking out nourishment
water, food and Earth's life force
Closer they come to the Centre
that molten seething cauldron
Spark - bright light - sears up the entwined ways
speeding faster, faster upwards
an energetic source pulsing through
coursing the route onwards
Contact - it touches the trunk
explodes into the wooden body mass
glowing, fluorescent, enlightening
fleeing along the arms
the network of branches vibrating
as each shred of light is experienced
some absorbed to heal and grow
more still to irradiate outwards
giving forth the wisdom of old
- touch this power, infuse its magic
now *you* are part of the spell
erudite in your knowledge
your task - to teach and to learn
your lessons will awaken others
and their learning bring you expansion
for we are all one
and have the Universe in our souls
heed the words of all Men
for even the greatest fool
can offer you the greatest insight
and so the tree begins our journey.

Giulia L Allsop

A VIEW OF MOW COP HILL

Mow is a hard-ribbed hill of millstone grit swept up from the plain
Where step by pace I can replace all that town days claim.

A thousand feet and more, above the unseen sea, She; and I
The nearest man in seven counties to the cloud crowded sky.

The horizon, round as a wheel from there, with Mow Cop hill the hub
That spins the sun-spoked farm fields where the sky's edges rub.

A peaceful high, breached only by the intercity train
Which hourly hauls from Manchester a sigh of distant rain.

The wind's song is Mow's song now but her pubs and parlours know
Once her heavens rang to the quarry hammer's blow

And sulphurous smoke choked her valleys and her people, choking, died
As counts in counting houses counted profits multiplied.

But where does it tell of this, those whose own ribs ached to breathe?
Where is the grateful monument, the unforgetting wreath

To all who came from dust to work the dust, to be paid in dust,
To be laid to dust, in service of a rich man's lust?

Against the breakers of this rock, whom this rock in turn near broke,
Stands a foolish mock castle, a vain and tasteless joke.

From a purse fat with privilege, a hat for old Bald Head,
An insult wrought of Mow stone, hollow as the bones of her dead.

Terry Fox

FEELING OLD AT XMAS

Xmas comes but once a year, definitely in December,
I used to know which day it was, but now I can't remember.
In days of old my hair was gold, and curly too I think,
But now there's just a wisp or two, the rest is rosy pink.

Jobs like tying up my laces used to be a piece of cake,
No problem mate, I'd bend right down, there wouldn't be an ache.
Glasses, well they weren't for me, my sight as keen as mustard
Pass the gravy will you dear; silly old fool, it's custard.

Things that were so full of life are wearing out quite fast,
Know what I mean, I thought you would, nothing's made to last.
Climbing mountains, running wild, fond memories of youth,
Xmas fare is here once more, and me without a tooth.

Mustn't grumble, could be worse, at least I have a pension;
I dream a lot, as well you know, of things I mustn't mention.
What really keeps me going, and with a zest for life,
Is having you my darling, my dear old 'trouble & strife'.

Jack Dyer

WINTER GALE

Siege from the elements -
uproar, riot, row!
Destroyer of calm, vandal from
the lowest depression.
Trespasser, hungry rogue
with mischievous frenzies of desire
to stir and rouse leaves,
to twist trees.
Ghost of the land,
poltergeist!
Ghost of the ocean,
sweller of heavy seas.
Tempestuous, passionate beast.

Rosalynn East

BLIND KINDNESS

Don't kill me with kindness,
It's a cruel thing to do.
Don't drain me with kindness,
Till I've nothing to do.
We all need to feel useful,
I know that you do,
But what have I got,
With someone like you.
You love and protect me from all outside,
We live in our safe little world.
No noise to upset, no emotion to jar.
You rush and you do,
and you say that's all right,
I'll do that dear, there's no need for you.
Don't you know I feel useless,
And it's because you're so kind.
Kindness becomes resented,
And that leads to feelings of guilt.
To resent someone's kindness,
makes one feel bad.
Feeling bad, feeling guilty, feeling useless,
and it's all done by kindness.
I hope I'm never so cruel,
Or so blind.

Christine Tedder

THE NIGHT WATCH

How still the night o'er No Man's Land, stark contrast to the day,
When Royal cousins' armies met, in wanton bitter fray.

So safe, this nocturne blanket, within whose folds I lie,
Visions of the day's events, manifesting in the sky.

Yon, blue eyed boy of eighteen years, just sixteen to his kin,
An unseen shadow behind a gun, his only mortal sin.

And what of Bill, the veteran, raw courage in his blood,
A hasty move, a flash, a bang, now ashes in the mud.

Pray, who'll miss Private Holden - a Quantock bride, they say,
No conscience had the 'Maxim', that blew their dreams away!

O'er there kneels Padre Caldwell, just cleric, truth to tell,
Fine letters written in the dark, of Sons who did so well.

Farewell sad world, with certainty, arms, no more to bare,
As unrequited peace, they've won, and bliss with Poppies, share.

Perchance to dream, I'll see again, red roses, round a door,
The open one that chapter closed, as home I left, for war.

Oh! To stroll that crooked lane, that ends in leafy bower,
And feast my eyes upon the May, in season's glorious flower.

This heady mead of homely thoughts, transcends each waking hour,
Rudely broken by the shells in savage shows of power.

A gaunt and wily Sergeant beckons 'stretchers' to the south,
A lucifer ignited 'fag', still hanging from his mouth.

The dulcet tones of Private Potts cascade along the trench,
Fine lyrics of some bawdy song, inspired by Brandy - French.

So, with sombre levity, the watch, as night, must end,
As chinks of light from an eastern sky, the darkened blanket rend.

Such days have dawned, such deeds are done, our future has been forged,
And from the cream of precious youth, vast channels have been gorged.

A fond farewell Oh Glorious ones, resplendent in this mire,
For we shall mourn the children, that you will never sire.

J R White

LAY DOWN AND DO NOT TALK . . .

Lay down and do not talk
just lay down and dream.
Make it clay and paper
and hair and ice, but
do not burn, we all hear
we hate to burn, and
listen to the cold that
is kissing at the window
and watch out for the car
that is waiting in the street
and make your hair neat
my love, for it is wet
and will freeze, and make
that drink neat my dear
for we cannot spare
the water, and listen
to the river
that will not move.

Daniel Bennett

MAY

Darkness dwells in May's old house.
Rain, like her tears, on the window pane.
May is unhappy and nobody cares,
The pain in her heart rips, shreds and tears.

Gone are the days of a young girl growing,
Eighty years have come to this;
By an empty fire-grate sewing,
Her birthday marked by no-one's kiss.

Too cold her pale, lily-white skin,
Too old her clothes and too thin,
Too cold the house a life to keep,
As she drifts on dreams to sleep.

Amy Fox (11)

PRESS DAY: A SONNET

'Pair in saucy office romance shocker!'
Is the headline in the gossip column
Relegating talk of crime and soccer
To the downpages of the humdrum.
There is more mileage in this love story
To tempt the news sense of our fellow hacks
In this world of tabloid Jackanory
Where scoops are needled out of old haystacks
With the aid of coffee and telephones.
'Hold the front page - forget council wrangle' -
They are more interested in our hormones
To find themselves an exclusive angle.
And, at the time the paper went to bed,
We joined it - in our private centrespread.

Jo Headley

SAINTS AND ANGELS

It's early in the morning
She's been talking all night
She waves her friends good-bye
And turns down the lights
She slowly climbs the stairs
To get ready for bed
The evening's conversation
Still flowing through her pretty head

And 'though she won't admit it
She sometimes feels a little scared
As she looks around her darkened room
To try to see what's there

But while the moon is high
It will watch you as you lie
And keep you 'til the morning brings its calm
For there's nothing there in the night
That's not there in the day-time
And you are far too beautiful to come to harm

But if these words don't warm you
And you find you still can't sleep
And you're haunted by every noise
Every whisper, every creak
If you need someone to lean on
Or you need a hand to hold
then you know I'm always here
To dry your tears, and keep you from the cold

So may all your thoughts be pleasant
And may all your dreams come true
And may the saints and angels,
While you sleep, watch over you.

Dave Guttridge

112

LEGALISED RAPE

It took twenty thousand acres of good land,
Enough to provide food for a town for a year.
It compulsorily purchased the homes of
Eleven hundred sparrows, fifty blackbirds,
Twenty foxes, twelve hundred rabbits,
Countless mice, butterflies and moths, and
Although it missed the church steeple
No work remained for a hundred people.

Pleasant lanes were blocked up, widened,
Narrowed, raised, lowered, re-aligned, spanned
By cold, grey concrete bridges, for all to see
This impersonal, tarmacadamed monster in all its
Dual carriaged, three laned, safety factored glory.

It cuts an hour off the journey from A to B.
So now you can get there in half the time
It took on the 'old dangerous roads.
But gone are the pleasures of travel
And the delights of the shady lay-by on the A49.

Through cutting, embankment, flyover and underpass
Runs this monument to our four-wheeled god.
Built by modern technology and the sweat of itinerate navvies.

It has eaten our land, the source of our food.
Left scars no landscape artist can ever improve,
Put blight on our hunting and shooting and courting,
And what does it give for our money supporting
Its conception birth and permanent nurture,
What return, interest or hope for the future?
Nothing more than the right to drive at 70 miles per hour
Through nowhere to our certain end.

James Meadows

MAN AND BOY

Warm flowing air encircles both
The dark, sparse, tall trunk
And the young, three foot high
Four year old sapling.

The sap rises but slowly
Through the old limbs.
The brain is dry as the skin, as the trunk.
Vision is hazy, hearing dim,
The voice vibrates loudly in chuckles.

The young one gazes up,
Sturdy alertness in posture and little face,
Small, wide nostrils eagerly absorb the air,
Smell, sound, sight are an entrancing mystery.

And the warm flow of air encircles both,
Touches in them a memory and premonition
Of over eighty years ago and eighty years hence,
Caught in the here and now,
The wheel for a moment stands still.

G Birke

LAST SECONDS

They said it was a job for life.
I guess they didn't lie.
A bob exploded, shrapnel flew,
Now I'm lying in a hospice,
But I guess they didn't lie.

Adrian Dowrick

A LOST LOVE NOT RETRIEVED

I shall not pass by this way again
For Life gives us just one chance,
And I have experienced sufficient pain
To warrant not returning!

I enjoyed our short and fun-packed time,
It gave my life a purpose.
But now our Love's a silent Mime
And our words have no more meaning!

I thought that we might rekindle yet
The spark of Love once known,
But perhaps it's better to forget
Than to dwell on that which was?

If there is an after-life
Where long-dead Lovers meet,
Then will be an end to strife
And we can love again!

Gerald I Law

LAST SUPPER

a woman
the table laden   prepared
the bread green   the plates dusty
apples with worms   cold tea   rancid butter
cutlery array & tarnished
the woman weeps   no-one comes

outside, traffic erasing tears, a whole world
a stranger's voice
'who is the woman locked in her house
& whom did she kiss?'
growing inaudible as swift fingers
turn up the radio

Nigel Walker

115

PARTICULARLY INDECISION IN A SMALL GARDEN

It *is*
green
and the grass is particularly
green,
(gardens in particular).
Wet it *is*
cool and knife-sharp
garden dreams
green dreams.
Grass cutting peculiar fingers.
Did you ever cut your finger on a piece of green?
On a sharp piece of green coolness?
And then lick it
wondering how green could be so sharp,
and red could be so salty.

Rachel Lee

HALF A CENTURY

The score is fifty, not yet out,
Still time to learn what it's all about,
The wicket stands - the bail's intact,
Now to plan how else to bat,
Do we stonewall - just play for fun?
Or take a risk and make a run.

As in life, the ball comes fast,
With little time to gain from life now past,
We lift the bat and make the stroke,
The rest consists of prayers and hope,
We make the runs, our hopes run high, -
What be the score before we die?

G West

COLLECTING FROGSPAWN AS A BOY

Eager, exuberant, wellingtons entering water with force that could harm
                                        some things
Waded: mud, decomposing leaves, twigs, weed, dense, putting slight rein
                                    around the rubber
Always some suddenly sodden socks, most likely mine
Do not recall net.
Jar, plastic bag
Far better, large tin, amount got
inside in one scoop. Super!
Recurrent urge to use just hands, a need to feel the stuff instantly,
                                       thoroughly,
Best moments, a thrillingly singular sensation
The substance, the action, surgery richly if not readily suggested
Spawn: upon transfer it sometimes slipping, splitting
In three little ponds enough to fill a bath
Embryos, tiny unborn eyeballs, some discoloured
Sludge white - death: bacterial, rampant excelling microbes, organic fire
Frogs: underwater as much as icebergs
Snatch attempts, successful, their throats, limbs, desperate
Aspiring Alcatraz of fingers against muscled ooze - frequent escapes
Kept two, Year, Vivarium
Fishtank for the fascinating spotted slop
Galaxy, mainly doomed to metamorphosis
Week, the black stars turned big commas
Fresh excitement

Ian Thomson

SWAN SONG

Proud and majestic billowing white, they sailed
The sea when the tide was high, invincible galleons
Turning slowly to look at each other. My pony
Would stand at the water's edge and stare,
And wonder that ships should dare
Come close to land just there.
But they always did, they were always there.
When the tide was out they would poke about or squat
On the marsh like cobbles, stranded, till water came lapping again.
When the tide returned they would sail away together.
     Now the cob is dead, we found him there
     Out on the salt marsh close by the sea,
     Ravaged feathers, rusty palled,
     Wanton deed of a cruel hand
     While vigilance pales in this beautiful land.

Elizabeth Mills

BANANAS VERSUS POETRY

Bananas appeal to me more than poetry.
Their simple uniformed appearance clashing
with the broad and diverse world of rhyme.
One begins life on a tree, bursting into
Existence, the other within the cruel, harsh depths
Of the poet's mind.

A poet contemplating the art of an
English tradition, while feasting
Upon a dreamy symbol of the exotic.
Maybe writing on an island beach
In the stifling heat would make poetry more fun
- or simply make bananas boring.

Clare Collison

NEW YEAR'S EVE

New Year's Eve had a great time.
Sat with the fire and a fag till four.
I said it wouldn't be the same as last time
And isn't 'cos the revelling is all next door.

The ham on the buns has gone curly,
I knew I was a fool to open all those crisps.
I might as well have gone to bed early
And put to sleep the hopes that I might be missed.

So I nursed a can of special till it went flat
And gathered up the old year like a hand of cards.
Pontificated at length on this and that
And supped the cup of solitude that went down hard.

As for resolutions you can stick them.
I never kept one up for more than twenty-four hours
The new year creeping like a vixen,
Stealing chicken hopes from our ivory towers.

But I wish you all a happy and a good one.
I hope the weather's kind and your wives are sleek.
And I hope you're not too overtly put upon
And as Burns said 'Lang may your lum reek.'

Brian S Boyd

A HEDONIST DREAM

The Sun sets down on the Cafe del Mar.
Laid-back nouveau hippies and natural
hedonists mingle and chill with a
cosmopolitan gathering, dealing out the night
force fuel. Party people from around the world
socialise ready for the night's surprise. Dressed
with style and sophistication. Neon lights draw
them towards another night of indulgence.
Beacons scan the black hills for elevated
souls, locking on and leading them onwards.

In a hyped explosion of celebration a
glorious band of drag queens, techno hippies,
glamsters, disco dandies, sex kittens and
hustlers, join forces on the dance floor
moving in time to the beat of a
Balearic base. Bodies gyrate, jerk, spin
contort and rotate in a blur of sweat
smoke and laser light. Passion for the
vibe is shared by all. Until the daystar
rises and the bodies find their space.

The Sun cleanses the Island of the
night's festivities. Tired souls make for
the seashore. Where bronze bodies lay
soaking up the healing rays of the day.

N G Rowland

FRANKLIN'S PROMISE

There will be a weeping and a wailing
And darkness will descend upon this place
Its people will be split down the middle
The dead shall rise and scream in their graves
And the evil that is with us shall transcend
The very fires of Hell and damnation
And all the evils of the pit shall torment the damned
Death is in the air and death is the air
But she is too clever
When I bite - I bite hard!
He says, unable to deliver
Oh God, why have you forsaken me?
To live in this world of cruelty, beauty, desire and death
I was but a child when my Mother was taken
To the long white corridor
Now she doesn't love me anymore
You let sleeping dogs lie
But now those dogs are dead
You've not long left yourself, my baby
September's Sapphire
And what affects my baby girl
You Slut! You Fiend!
The dawn will not be yours!
The rape of life my sweet sixteen
Oh sweeping, flowing, smoothly, would I take your breath
Your eyes are cold as the fires of Hell
You are but a child:
Too young to see the evil that you do,
The evil that you bring
And the evil that you are.

Desirée Paull Merriden

THE ENFIELD OAK

The towering oak stands majestically, hands reaching for the sky,
It's stood for many years, and it's watched the world go by.
It's weathered many winters and the storms have left their mark,
But this planet's roughest weather couldn't break the stout oak's heart.

If the tree could only talk it would have such tales to tell,
But though it watches everything, it keeps its secrets well.
It's witnessed many changes in its sedentary life,
It's seen the passing years and it's watched the world in strife.

Countless lovers courting, it's heard them laugh and cry,
It's witnessed tender meetings and seen the tearful goodbye.
Though keeping the same sure silence that it has held so long,
I'm sure the oak could tell us all where we are going wrong.

Sad to think the oak will still be there when I am gone,
But glad to think it's watching still as this world carries on.

Dee Johnson

THE LONELY NIGHT

I keep my nightly vigil
Alone am I awake?
As pearls of silence hang
In the velvet dark.

Moonlight etches the world
In shades of black and white.
A beam of lamplight sprinkles
Dewdropped trees with diamonds.

Rainwashed streets swirl
With rivers of silver,
And all this treasure
I would surrender
For one loving word.

Mary Hunter

TERMINATION OF THE SOUL

In a world with little sorrow,
Where the children tumble and cry,
And the land lies torn and forgotten,
The Past lives left to die.

The embryo of a new child,
Lies still in the mother's womb,
It cannot hear the death threats,
From within its tightened tomb.

As the termination takes hold the child of 5 lays near
The child watches on as the mother lays in sweat
And the man hounds the door to collect the unpaid debt

As the mother writhes in agony,
The cries of the child are heard
And the embryo curls up,
Never to hear the bird.

Yet another cannot wait,
To see the new life through,

As the embryo's horizons fade,
And the mother's thoughts grow dim,
Nobody is there to comfort,
The tiny child Tim.

As the mother weakens she whispers in his ear,
And the face turns to horror as hunger strikes with fear.

Little Tim is left to face the world,
Without a guiding life,
He walks out into the world,
His burden heavy with strife.

The arms of a stranger takes his life in hand
Kill the very brain inside and bury him in the land.

G Parker

WHITBY, NINETY THREE

Cold, bone cold, in the cemetery
As the kippered old sailor
Was lowered; pretending he was dead.

His widow thinking all the time
Of the insurance and the parlour
Meats. Would the vicar come?

The wind snatched at the hats
And macs of his grim faced
'There but for fortune' mates.

You hurried by lest they
Should think you were some
Kind of nut; a funeral freak.

The familiar ritual was conducted swiftly,
Gulls in chorus; soon it
Was all over bar the whispering.

Angela Stone

CLOUD ON THE HILLS

High in the hills the dragons sleep,
stretched out along the steepest fells
like great contented cats.

Hidden, they lie beneath the turf,
among the rockfalls and the braided trees.
Their long curved backs and folded wings
outlined against the Border sky.

One day they may awaken,
emerging from their chrysalis of grass and rock
to gaze with cold reptilian eye upon the scattering sheep,
and make their plans to rule the world . . .

R E Hull

INCONSEQUENTIAL MONOLOGUE

i haven't spoken
to anyone today

not a single word
to a single soul

i don't mind though
'cos i can talk to myself

i went out
for a walk earlier

it was raining
i said to me

you're mad
not out loud of course

'cos then i probably
would be mad.

G Hayward

THE TEN CYCLEMENTS

Don't hike, ride a bike
Don't push, pedal a chain
Don't fly, take a trike
Don't stand, sit on a saddle
Don't smoke, burn your rubber
Don't wash, oil your parts
Don't puff, pump it hard
Don't crawl, change the gear
Don't steal, use titanium
Don't die, wear a helmet

Simon Adams

UNTITLED

To dream a dream of perfection
Where all is safe and sound
No people starving. No barren ground
Where fact is fact, a spade a spade
Where from the sun one needs no shade
But then in all perfection, sudden thought
All one would have to do is as one ought
And there is missing the vital element
Man as human likes green grass twice as much as he likes cement.
To call a spade a spade he may
But only to his friends dismay
As in the event of passing by
Another man's feelings, all must cry
Against perfection as much as I
For though we strive this aim to gain
Man imperfect is not such strain
As we who let our feelings show
Better off we feel you know
After a stumble a loving kiss
Not much seems here amiss
But really isn't it better after all
Not to have to reach too high
As he who does is sure to fall
We're only human after all.

M M Walton

IN THE EAST

Exotic foods on roadside stalls,
Colourful garments, household tools,
The sound of money changing hands,
Some gambling men are making plans

A sea of bikes, thousands of faces,
Wise old women selling laces,
The temple, a haven from the noise,
A ping-pong table for the boys

Concrete towers surround the parks,
Men with cages, sparrows and larks;
Statues and fountains still remain
And sloping roofs made out of cane

Evening comes, there's a restaurant here,
Smell of soya and bottled beer,
Some army lads are looking brave,
A flaming wok and glasses raised

No-one's sure quite whom to trust,
The noodle dish is still a must;
So many streets I'll never roam,
The visa says it's time for home

Anthony Hunt

WHAT SHOCKS YOU

What shocks you? Dead gull in its blistered wreath
of seaweed? No, I have to call you back
The Viking Sea gives you the screw and rack
A twig will do to ascertain it breathes

Not even when you tunnel in the sand
And worm through amber chambers into dung
Still warm and sticky like a buried lung
You do not mind, I have to wash your hands

Was I like this? I won't go to the shore
With bare feet, I'm a sentinel estranged
Upon a beach towel. In the sea you changed
A tiny pulsing of the waves, no more

Afraid than wood, than water. Armed with fear
I snap it onto you so lungs will flap
Up like a panicked gull one wing collapsed
When ruthless waves like bogeymen appear

To swallow you. And yet I brag you're brave
Unto the other mothers. Brutal girl
Trusting the world so blindly my blood curls
Up into love, my sweating need to save.

Rachel Parker

INTERMENT

We cluster around this inverted cube;
waiting for the man in his shabby black
suit to pick his careful way round paths
and plinths and dreams of other ways back.

The wife in stilettos, the daughter
with heels scuffed in her school shoes,
the son, now fatherless trying to fathom
out what is expected of him, whose

life should he live now? The grandmother
torn between anger and desperation,
broken on the rock of her faith in
a jealous god so full of contradictions.

The words are said, but not heard,
the last remains' - what a euphemism
for a six-foot complex of disarray
now powdered into the final schism -

are lowered awkwardly, absurdly
followed by a clump of earth, a rose;
in limbo we neither go nor stay, where
he is, where we are, no-one knows.

Ron Parker

MORNING GLORY

She gazes at me through windows,
Considers herself unseen
Through her glassy screens.
I trade on that; amuse myself
As I take my daily bath which she
Prepares for me each morning
For her own delight.

I hesitate, cock my black head
As she expects me to
Checking for dangers
From bushes and trellises
then, one last, slow swivel,
I plunge and wallow and splash
Knowing she watches me
Binoculared still.

My wings shower sunlit drops all over
Everywhere; radiating rainbows
For our mutual pleasure.
I do not hurry, I take my time;
Stretch - quiver in the wetness
Of the morning and spread
My body on the grass.
And still she watches.

My partner, who knows her place
Stays silent on the fence,
Waits for the moment to descend
And take my space to use
What I have left for her.
I begin to smooth and preen
Ready to start another shining day.

Rita Watts

VISIONS UNLIMITED

Wishing abatement of time, or to regress is beyond any power
To stop tomorrow to-day and then return to a particular hour
Is to dream of that moment which seems merely just passed
An alternative? Now it has gone out of retrievable grasp.

Is it wise to reflect? Sometimes, many times it is beyond any power
To subdue uncontrollable thoughts desirous of an elapsed hour
To dream of a 'yester-eve' and desperately pray it was this time
Has been his. Often been hers. And has most certainly been mine.

Are resolutions strong enough to withstand beyond any power
More often the space of endurance is measured solely by the hour
Which ultimately means the recurring of a familiar favourable reverie
Approving with quiet expression, willpower is surpassed temporarily.

To strive against conflict between then and now is beyond any power
So why resist? When submission is to afford pleasure in a past hour
For a fantasy is harmless, relaxing and occasionally makes you realise
Harnessing a dream may be possible with effort or an amount of
                                                            compromise.

To relinquish the ability of random dreaming is perhaps not beyond any
                                                            power
But to do so would be unfortunate and sad to abandon a noteworthy hour
Let us therefore endeavour to remain unceasingly constant, musers us all
Grateful for these diversions. Pensive interludes. Always at hand to recall.

Freida A W Haggart

UNEMPLOYED

A naked bulb hangs overhead
In a squalid, grimy squat.
Grief-shaken, in a corner,
A girl lies, smoking 'pot'

A pounding Reggae beat hangs still,
Upon the ambient air.
Discarded needles, rusting, lay.
She groans, but doesn't care.

She's waiting for a stronger 'fix'
But the 'pusher' on the street,
Demands a higher price each time,
With a deadline she can't meet.

Luminous despair despair now shines,
From haunted, hollowed eyes.
Lucifer's in that tainted smoke,
Her lonely soul, His prize.

Her slender arms are pricked and scabbed.
Her life lies wasted, arid, sere.
Sad academic, unemployed,
With death her new career.

Marjorie Chapman

SUMMER SONG

I love the lilt of Summertime,
When all my thoughts turn into rhyme.
Every sound a subtle beat,
Thrushes sing and sparrows cheep.

There's music in the Summer breeze,
That gently whispers through the trees.
Shaking weeping willows tall,
Hark I hear the blackbird call.

The pitter pat of Summer rain,
Softly beats on my window pane.
Dancing clouds in clear blue sky,
Like charioteers go riding by.

Grasshoppers click in grasses high,
Kestrels squeal then dive on prey.
Rippling cobs on corn tops wheeze,
While bulrush crackles on sultry breeze.

Breaking the still of a Summer's night,
The owl hoots loud then starts in flight.
Lively bats like mice with wings,
Disturb the night when church bell rings.

Summer lightning thunderous clatter,
Graceful swans glide on the water.
An orchestra plays all season long,
The lilt and sounds of a Summer song.

Mary P Linney

UNITED IN GREED

The missionary weeps with the dead child in his arms
What once was paradise has lost its worldly charms
The water hole is empty and plague covers the land
But the big boys at the UN will never understand

The doctor tends the boy with a bullet in his leg
He's rush him to hospital but there are no empty beds
The boy has lost his home, his family and his friends
He prays to God each night that today's the day war ends

The aid worker despairs as the hungry people plead
Because he has no food but a thousand mouths to feed
Ethnic cleansing has brought chaos to this land
While the UN sit and wash the blood from their hands

The United Nations can impose sanctions
Or they can send in the troops
And if you're lucky and have oil wells
Then they can jump through hoops
But if your country holds no value
then they are tied up in red tape
They make noises of disapproval
While armies plunder, kill and rape.

Paul Lagdon

KEEP YOUR 'AIR ON

'Get your ruddy 'air cut yelled the corporal loud and clear,
'With that silly jungle on your 'ead, I'm surprised that you can 'ear'
'And on parade termorrer morning, if its not cut short and trim,
I'll 'ave your guts for garters and your life will be grim!'

So when we finished for the day, I joined a lengthy queue
Outside a Blackpool barber's shop with other lads in Air Force blue.
After what seemed like eternity, I emerged shaken and forlorn
And felt Winter's icy breezes where my curly locks were shorn.

Then upon inspection by my two-striped lord and master,
He scrutinised me balefully which made my heart beat faster,
But I was 'Bulled' up to the eyebrows and felt quite debonair
Till he whispered 'Am I 'urting you? 'Cos I'm standing on your 'air.'

'Get your bleedin' 'air cut' he screamed at me again,
I thought 'Here goes another sixpence down the blinking drain',
That evening, at the barber's I said 'Shave it all away,
At least I'll save my money and stop myself going grey.'

Next morning my tormentor snarled 'You look like a bloomin' pig
You'll 'ave to save your pay lad and buy yourself a wig.
This really was the final straw, I began to wish that he was dead
So I scalped that blasted corporal and stuck *his* hair upon my head!

John Martin

PISS HEAD POET

They say you wrote a thousand words a day
Try as I might I still have my doubt
To me you were that drunken lout
Maybe you had something profound to say
Like an old dog you only went one way
In the village pub with your pint of stout
'It's time lads all out'. The landlord would shout
And you standing up, so pissed would sway

Outside in the alley you bend over double
Up and out comes the stout, guinness and all
But all I can do is hope for the rain
For you are my father's father trouble
I remember once you were so proud and tall
But now your son's son can see all your pain

C P Andrews

WOMAN

You
are my doorway to madness,
you
are my river to sanity.
Nemesis
of my heart
you weave your spells
through chimerical thoughts
drawing them to fragile fineness.
My mind is an instrument
on which you play
your games.
Most of all
you
are woman.

Albert E S Gamage

MINOR COUNTY SOUTH

Here December holds no fears, makes no threat:
Though businessmen stay snug in thatched extensions
And clean the clubs that ease their summer tensions,
We countrymen know it isn't winter yet.

The man who drives the tractor's from the city:
Sometimes he wonders why those white birds walk behind.
He loathes the job, but it was all that he could find
And now he's stuck with it, the more's the pity.

The local horsey-set trot through the pasture;
Wear silly clothes, shout silly thing, trot on.
Giggling girls bounce big, jodhpured arses upon
Old broken horses - all they'll ever master.

Beside the motorway the shotguns thunder;
The year's first home-reared pheasants hit the ground . . .
Only in the country are all such to be found:
Man the toiler; man the thinker; man the hunter.

Ashleigh John

A SAD STORY

I will tell you a sad story,
And the man listened,
And he told the woman,
Who told the boy,
Who told the girl,
Who told her mother,
Who late one night told her husband,
Who told his lover,
Who when visiting told her grandmother,
And when her grandmother was alone, she wept,
And told no-one . . .

Joy Reeves

REDUNDANCY

My life smashed
My self-esteem gone.
My job taken away
My purpose for living disappearing.

A blow dealt out to the whole of my being
Like a death blow
A violent punch to my stomach
A slap in the face that makes me reel.

My confidence seeps away
I withdraw into my shell
Speak when I am spoken to
- And watch television.

I flick through the papers
Looking at the adverts
No jobs for me!
Don't fit the bill.

Some friends avoid me
Not knowing what to say
Others give suggestions
About how I use my day.

The forms, the questions,
The signing on,
The restart, the job club
And training for new work.

But where is this new work?
Where are these jobs?
Where will I go
When I can't find a job?

Gill Sathy

LADIES COMPETITION DAY AT MENDIP GOLF CLUB (IN WINTER)

Frozen fingers, running nose,
Feeling cold from head to toes,
Fog comes down, I cannot see
But on I go relentlessly.
Clubs on back (can't use my trolley)
Rain comes down - forgot my brolly.
Tears are running down my cheek,
I think my eye has sprung a leak.
My bobble hat keeps blowing off
I'm bound to get a cold or cough,
But I must keep going - I could win you see
If all the rest are worse than me.
On hole 8 and not a par,
Oh well I'll eat my chocolate bar
'Twill give me strength and keep me frisky
But I'd much prefer a tot of whisky.
Down the 9th the wind's so strong
Glad I've got my thermals on.
My score is rising at alarming rate,
The par is 5 and I take 8.
Only two more holes to go,
Having fun? - The answer's *"no"*.
Game is over, battle done
My total score is 101
Nett 82 - well I did try hard,
Just enough strength left to tear up my card.
I'm back in the nice warm Clubhouse.
And now I'm completely unwound,
I really must say, although it's been a bad day,
I can't wait 'til I play my next round.

Marjorie Roberts

SOMEONE TO CARE FOR

I watched him almost wither
In the sunny dozing evening
An outstretched hand visibly shaking
Like a delicate leaf in the nudging wind

Swiftly eyeing his cardboard introduction
'Homeless and hungry'
People hurried home, probably hungry
Recoiled by his rancid smell
Equally anti-social his flea-ridden clothes
'Could you spare some change, please?'
The words eased gently from his hair-ravaged face
I studied him hard as a tourist snapped him
With her Sony then walked off giggling

'Could you spare some change, please?'
A city gent brusquely walked up to him
Arrogant by virtue of an easy life
'I have to work to have the good things in life' he spat
His victim's eyes glanced up
Like the blooming of a beautiful flower
For his eyes were blue, deep, deep, sparkling, mischievous blue
His ravaged outer appearance an insult to his spirit

The city gent walked off, he sat alone
He too wanted the good things in life
a bed, some warmth and food
And someone to care for

Shane White

THE SYSTEM

It's not that I'm lazy
And I do need a job
But I can't see me slogging
For just a few extra 'bob'

I'm strong and I'm healthy
And I'm pretty well fed
My rent is paid for me
And I have a good bed

I've tried out this working game
A number of ways
But never could stick it
Because of the money it pays

Now there's a job going
That pays 'time and a bit'
But why should I bother
to climb out of my 'pit'

So I don't think I'll bother
To go out looking today
And anyway. Why should I work
when the system will pay.

Charles Omer Desjarlais

THE ETERNAL NOTE OF SADNESS

They live in a world
That abuses gender,
Because individuals are just part of the mass.
With those who drink heavily
To drown their brains
Against the illusion,
That life is pure, innocent and safe.
Against the Conformists,
The establishment, Big Brother.
Against the silence driving everyone mad,
With the beggars, murderers and the persecuted
Racing against atoms of uranium
In Countries, where the dying
Count the hovering vultures
Looking upon the creeping desert
With people that have no heart
The Deprived?
The safety light in the exit door
Has been taken out.

Victoria E Coe

THE SILENT STORMS

I feel the silent storms between us
Crashing on my shores,
And friendship seems as far apart
As the sea and skies could be.

The seas reach out to touch the skies
The clouds evades the waves,
Strange. I hear the silent storms between us
Stridently stark and stern.

Charlette de Christi

BREAKING TO BLUE

There is a stillness about this day
sky grey as tempered steel,
ripples idly washing the bank,
year plumed cygnets resting
silent on water.

Ours was such a day,
open to a whitened world,
first call of winter, hard chill frost,
when our times were free.

I remember those days
as we held them, first call of being
frail as summer's butterflies
now in grief forever lost,

as mace spikes burst
filling space with downy seeds,
flying thoughts carried away
on winds of the mind.

I keep them still, locked away
as image in memory fades
warming again as sky breaks to blue.

Elizabeth Mayne

THE FINAL EVENING OF THE VISIT

Gentle water tickling the stones on the foreshore
provided a subtle background to our tired but eager
activity. The disco over, the coach trip home tomorrow
Ever-present in our minds, we threw roundéd pebbles into
the brine.

Daylight had gone, twilight had abandoned us and so we
searched for skimming-stones by distant shore-lights,
yellow, white and green. Bent double, like the French
harvesters of oysters, we scanned the waters edge; like
Olympic discus-throwers we spun our hopes over the
teasing waters. One, two, three, four bounces, - we
listened carefully. No other noises except those of
youngsters playing, paddling, enjoying the moment in
groups-distant. The true beauty of the scene has been
missed and squandered by those enthusiastic children.

The hot chocolate of our civilisation awaited us.
For a while the Arethusa and school were far away: we
had perceived the timeless enchantment which had inspired
mankind from first-born present.

It is haunting scene which can never be captured and,
hopefully, never be forgotten.

Stephen Bristow

A COLLAGE OF THOUGHTS AND MEMORIES

April 26th 1994

Daytime streams
in through the
glass and it is
A shining Tuesday
14.58 pm style.
Here, random
quadrants of this
wood-boarded,
floorboard floor
are drowned in the
shining, glue-like,
milk of the sun.
Green and crows,
the areas of our
fields are smooth
in the painted
melody of
mid-afternoon day.
The satellite's kiss,
along with the
breath of her
hazy spring ceiling
on the wind.
Live this way,
Live this way,
and feel
valuable.

Andrew James Napier

A WALK INSIDE MY HEAD

When I cannot sleep at night, and toss round in my bed,
I pass the long long hours all right
With a walk inside my head.

I start round Tesco's meat and fish and readimeals galore,
I plan each meal, each day, each dish
Prepared the day before.

Then Sainsbury's pass before my eyes with food of many nations.
They've pizza, pasta, curry too -
Good job we're not on rations.

I make my lists and plan my route all ready for the morrow,
But in the morn it's all a blur,
I'm blank, much to my sorrow.

Still, never mind, the night will come -
It Asda now be said,
The Safeway to a Kwik-Save night
Is a walk inside my head.

Cindy Wall

UNTITLED

In his room-records,
a pork pie hat,
eyes fixed,
occupation hope,
used to be so cool,
with my looks,
now - sit and stew,
bathe everyday,
locked limbs, thoughts as I woke,
Kicks, I was old.

Gary Malt

MESS ROOM MEMORIES

Dartboard hanging on the wall
Card games round the table play
'Tea's up' there came the call
How I long for here to stay

Fruit machines with reels spinning
Social club outings by the score
Oh what happy times from the beginning
Soon to be lost for evermore

Where oh where their smiling faces
Mingling crowds voices loud
Gone to different places
Drifting aimlessly like a cloud

As I peer through the shattered pane
Behold the mess therein
Its sacrilege quite insane
The perpetrators of this sin

The faceless ones our fate did seal
The kiss of death this place now bears
The wound so deep, too deep to heal
The floor so wet with our tears

R G E Castleton

WINTER SOLSTICE

A biting North Wind, rattling window panes all day,
Battered crows fluttering in the tree tops,
And snatched swirling smoke from chimney pots.
The Icy Blast roared and tore past tight closed doors:
It tormented wild beasts at large upon the Moors
With showers of hailstones, tumbling from skies of slate grey.

Through the brief day's hours, Robins whistled plaintive song,
And starved Kittywakes screeched and rode
The wind above fields where cattle lowed.
From Gully, Stream and Ditch, water ran in full spate.
From roadside drain came hiss and gurgle, 'neath the grate'
Rushing water sounded everywhere, the day long.

The short day struggled hard to keep the dark at bay:
Until dusk closed in again at four,
When 'The Long Night' gripped the land once more.
While Bird and Beast and Man sought shelter from the cold,
Scudding cloud, chased by a half-moon above the wold,
Hid fleeting stars and patches of the Milky Way.

Then Orion's Starry Glory flashed into view
Amongst the Zodiac; Club on high.
Winter's Glittering Jewel of The Night Sky,
The Hunter and his Dog, wheeling round Polaris.
The darkened land in limbo through the Solstice,
Shivered, slept or hibernated: 'The Long Night' through.

The Ancients burned great bonfires all through this long night,
And remembered The Old Year's Passing
With Fire and Dance; then Praying.
They Believed, with Trust, The Sun's returning power
Would light and warm the land again, for The Sower:
Whose husbandry brought forth Harvest at Summer's Height.

G Fisher

DUM DUM LAND

It's dum dum land come join the happy throng even past midnight
radios blast out a song,
Where cars should be parked there is only litter which makes
law abiding residents all feel bitter,
Yes dum dum land could be a pleasant place, instead gaze around
it's a damn disgrace,
Residents of all colours and creeds think their gardens are to only
grow weeds,
To hear the language the children use would certainly make you blush,
They come from broken homes say the teaching staff that is why they cuss,
Perhaps an alibi should be made for me, as I survey the scene and sip
my tea,
My expectations are far too high, twenty years in dum dum land and I can
only sigh,
Maybe it's time to move out of the real world and find ourselves a new
home,
But I will always think of dum dum land no matter where we roam.

Dennis Roy Judd

REGRET

The wind blows
Through plans
Made, forgotten,
Unfulfilled.
The life pans
Out. The fallen
And the killed,
And the wind blows.

Mark Reid

REFURBISHING

Her wedding ring had worn quite thin
Looking after him
Between the Anniversary Waltz
And all the other dances he had led her through.

Such fragile things to wear so thin.
But wedding rings, like marriage vows
She later learned to her regret,
Were not substantial.

Like a razor slash of deep intent,
The bloodied knuckle, torn skin;
She emptied all her life with him
Upon the counter of a jewellery store.

Make it wider was her plea
Make it easier to dance with.
The finger healed, yet left a scar.
But now they dance to celebrate
A ring refurbished, a second chance.

T Nesbit

SPECIAL DELIVERY

By pilot-boat they came,
From the home-port of Tyne.

In the roads at midday our vessel lay,
Eyes intent towards the pierheads gazed.
Familiar launch - 'Hadrian' - a bone in her teeth
Brought a smile; She's on her way!

A waving hand, small behind the windshield's glare
Made certain the hope; She is there!

Upstretched hands from the heaving deck
Raised the token, as eyes met
And understood.
In plastic bag, with 'papers for the crew,
The floral blooms gave their message clear.

'I wanted to bring you something
You don't see on ships . . .'

Fresh flowers now the cabin grace,
In the shaving glass - the only place.
A gift of home, from Home.

T J Boult

THE MUSICIAN

Be not so proud, dear lady,
      In your green and gold brocade.
Pleats will soften, laces fray
      And colours slowly fade.

Your ardent suitors soon will pass
      In careless cavalcade,
One at the joust, one in his cups
      And more in the far Crusade.

All of you now remembered no more
      Than sparrows under the eaves,
Save by one lowly musician
      Who loves and dreams and grieves.

His instrument and even his name
      Have vanished like autumn leaves
But his melody makes you immortal still
      As the lovely Lady Greensleeves.

C W Hill

BLACK GOLD

Blackened corpses marked for death
the oil pollutes the living breath.
Anguished cry, unheeded call
the innocent around us crawl.
Blackened earth devours the dead
no more creatures there have fed,
into the sea the dust and bone
all new life killed in the womb.
Once again the power wheel starts,
once again the earth it marks,
so as the deadly taint appears
let the image again renew your fears.

Angie Howard

NIGHT FLOWER

She wanted more than this
Felt someone should've saw her
She's used to this sort of thing

The world will go up in a shriek of silence
Of silence you kept and tried to hide from her

Lucky sisters
Living each other's lives
Staring through one pair of eyes
One soft glare
Sensing every torch-delicate pleasure

Night escape, so dark and cool
if only I could do this
Ghostly I drift
No focus - just a gaze

Kamikaze girl
Keep your distance
She won't invite me to her celebrations
Some party!

Starting now
A red plush
At last some concentration
Millions of lights in my skull
Flashing and being crushed in my hand
More liquid velvet

Julie Ann Devon

UNCLE NORMAN

Uncle Norman
Witnessed an accident once.
Blood everywhere.
He said it was
The worst day of his life,
Except for the day
When he met Aunt Ethel,
For forty years his wife.
But Norman would joke,
Not the sort of bloke
To take things seriously.
Nothing phased Norman,
Except when Ethel died.
'Lost everything now' he said,
And then he cried.
He'll get a good send-off tomorrow.

Tony Jones

COUNTRY BREATH

Grab a handful of dirt
      Let your senses roam,
Feel the bark of a tree
      Let the elements lash you;
Try to crush a stone, touch the air
      Or squeeze a handful of H_2O.
A barometer of life
      At harmony with the earth,
Let your head imbibe
      The exhilarating freshness;
For soon the soil is acid,
      The tree dead, the stone sand,
The air poisoned, the water polluted
      And the world void.

J R Minty

MY WAY HOME

Long years I have wandered far from here,
Over mountains steep, and barren plains
Old castles rare, near sunlit shores
But the west of England lured me back again
With wooded vales and heathered heights.
Deep streams wandering out of sight
Awakened warmed by morning sun,
That shines on beauty wild, unspoilt winding path,
Where hamlets' peace, where men for ages past have toiled,

Mysterious woods hide shy, wild deer.
Then poised for flight, they are so near
Land far away may beckon me
Exotic places, Land and Sea.
Those sun-drenched islands, domes and spires
Of homely cottages, farms and byres.
The wooded hills, the rushing stream,
All those are woven in my dream.
But when I awake, I need to be
Always with those most dear to me
Material things and travelled seas
My husband gives me love and peace.

A B Hopkins

DEAR ALICE . . .

We shared teddy bears and jelly tots
We shared our nursery rhymes
We learned to read and write our names,
To count, and tell the time.

The time that passed as we grew up
Together, sharing all.
We played and learned together,
Went to college after school.

We looked for love, found broken hearts,
We wiped each other's tears.
Exchanged our darkest secrets,
Swapped our hopes, our dreams, our fears.

And now they call us *grown ups*
We've reached maturity,
Our lives are full of jobs and work
Responsibility.

But in between the bustle
I save some time to spend,
To sit and write a letter
To my dearest, oldest friend.

Melanie Anne Hamilton Davies

THE STORM

The sky released a roar
  As it was stabbed by a jagged light
A moment of searing brightness
  Devoured by the black of night.
The raindrops thundered to the ground
  As if thrown by a demon hand
And joined together with one thought
  To drown this innocent land

The wind with the voice of a tormented soul,
  Could only twist and turn
A beast with new-found freedom
  Not knowing which way to run.
It lashed and whipped its insane course
  Across the valley floor
Behind it lay destruction - the village lay before.

The choir of bells in the wooden church,
  The warning for all to hear,
Rang out but could not pierce the minds
  Of a town paralysed with fear.

With no warning or tell-tale signs
  The holocaust had begun
Heaven h ad suddenly darkened her brows
  And the deathly terror was on
And when, at last, Mother Nature's wrath
  Was spent and all was calm
The havoc wreaked in that chosen place
  Only God would understand.

H G McHattie

THE NUMBERS GAME

Finger of fortune, finger of fate
Please point at me before it's too late

My problem first started upon the day
The National Lottery I started to play

At first it seemed to be just good fun
It didn't really matter to me who won

So lucky numbers and birthdates I started to pick
I had every confidence that they'd do the trick

Now off to my Lottery outlet my money to pay
I'm all ready now this new game to play

I watched my selections placed into the slot
Please finger of fortune, let my numbers be 'hot'.

'Saturday Night Fever', eyes glued to the telly
My palms are all wet, my body's like jelly

The Lottery drum churns - just like my tummy
Finger of fate please send me some money

It's all a big letdown - no happy smile
It seems all my numbers have missed by a mile

The following weeks have gone just the same
Why oh why am I playing this game?

Oh finger of fortune, finger of fate
Please point at me before it's too late

I'm getting quite desperate, just a tenner will do
Please point at me, please say - 'It's you.'

John Marshall

QUESTIONS

(The murder of Jamie Bulger)

Did unformed perception of celluloid images
transform a prurient fiction into fact
so that warped, emboldened curiosity
could wish for a single, verifying, task?
Thus, linked to form a mindless, monstrous unity
did they choose such scenes to re-enact?

In aftermath,
did they desire enhancement or cover,
by mingling of bright paint with blood?
Or did it seal, for evermore, an evil
too easily released in turbulent flood?

Or are those to blame,
whose brightly tempting visions
such deceptively flimsy webs so darkly spin,
that they coat in adult blood lust
childish reason still punily developed,
warped and thin?

And, was it by expression of such sick imagination
that the weft of civilisation came undone,
and two sickly, undeveloped souls enjoining
in horrid violence, could perform as one?

Tell me now, that I am wrong for weeping,
not just for Jamie's brief extinguished light,
but that such cold evil could be roused from sleeping
frosting two more lives with deadly blight.

Sheila Sharpe

THE BETRAYAL

The truth dies in decayed mouths,
Entangled by a web of deceit;
Storm clouds gather on a treacherous night
As dark deeds beckon where there is no light.
Coins jingle in a traitor's belt
            under electric skies,
As knaves and vagabonds are thrown together
For an orgy of destruction and betrayal,
Honesty is sorely amiss.
Stolen by a traitor's kiss.
And a king waits for the wind of death,
As Roman hyacinths blossom under murderous breath.
Sleeping men awake to clashing swords,
And harsh words, when words are useless,
Clashing with a pre-ordained plan
As Calvary beckons the chosen man
Hearts sting like nettles underfoot
As disciples fly into the night,
Yet one conspirator knows it isn't right
When a man of grace is taken in disgrace
Imprisoned in an alien place
Scorned and goaded with disdain and hate
painfully aware of eventual fate.
When bracelets of hair mingle with thorned flesh,
Adding to sadistic delight
'Tis now the very witching time of night
When churchyards yawn and hell itself breathes
As free men are made slaves
So that all men are freed.

Anthony James McLoughlin

READING ABOUT LADAKH IN THE FALCON

I sit in the hotel bar in my executive loneliness
Chit chat chit chat.
Around me other products of a society dedicated to assertive
achievement and business fat.
Some sit alone slowly completing the intake of high inducing
stress reducing
comfort
drawn from the cigarette.

And yet
I read about another world as far away as the moon but as near as
my feet.
Another life - alien but full of sensitivities.
It makes me whisper 'of course'
I look around.
I don't feel superior or privileged,
but I know there is little in common
between me and the other lives
that cross in this temporary homestead.
I go to bed.

Mary Wilde

SHEFFIELD EXODUS

In the heather-clad splendour of Peakland
You can abseil or you can climb
(Beside the ten thousand others
Who turn up at the very same time.)

You can walk along in the country
Communing with Nature and God
(With a bevy of fidgeting school-kids
And a string of excitable dogs.)

You can picnic al fresco at Stanage
- Or Lose Hill or Mam Tor, instead,
(With a dozen or so paragliders
Paragliding about round your head.)

No, Sundays are no longer tranquil,
The church and the dinner are gone,
And those who aren't Meadowhall-shopping
Are swelling the countryside throng.

E Caiger Gray

DEATH ON THE A1

He stops, stares and waits,
Feels and breathes the embers in the snow,
The crimson veins and silken threads,
That ebb from her body,
Lying without a shroud.

Entwined as one, he circles his mate,
Silent now, without the gift of life,
Her body embracing the ice-touched ground,
That joins the features,
That once stood proud.

And with solemnity, he bows his head,
As the mourners gather, as the curtains close,
No plate of ham or funeral tea,
The last rites sound,
And silently he leaves.

Nigel Dobson

BETRAYAL

White hands that used to comfort me
Now old, with gnarled knuckles curved
Like witches' claws
Hard working hands, now soft and pale
But with the hidden strength of steel
Fill me with dread
Blank eyes of fades grey
Now blaze with a demonic glare
That scorch my soul
The gentle face that I once loved
Contorted now with hate
To haunt my dreams

A tide of tears, to wash away
The pain of hidden bruises.
Shameful secrets buried deep.
Almost forgotten.

But while I sleep
The monsters of my mind
Come out to play.

Grace Sim

UNTITLED

These wintry days
wind tears icily
through huddled clothes
to shivering helplessness
and everything rushes
in adrenaline light
insane with meaninglessness
and while I stumble on
I dream with longing
of distant remembered summer
in deep forgotten countryside
days of languor
yawning with dawn
glistening dew and radiant colours
paling to heat and light of noon
and the collapsed slowed time
of early afternoon
eyes follow shade
swaying so gently
in slithering breeze
mesmerising motion
of sheer, lonely existence
so little really matters
when there is time
for reflection and contemplation
in long hours of stillness
and immersing silence.

Andrew Elsby

THE PRESS

They want to iron our dreams. Straighten us out,
Make us them.
Press our minds with naked lies - libels, liable
To expose the banal.

Giggly girls of page three with paper-thin heads
Making tits of whom? Unbecoming Stars with nothing
On - and nothing changing under the Sun.

The void reflected with a Mirror-image of tired and
Trendy complacency.
'X'press-es trying to impress, Prizes, Prizes, Prizes,
Never surprises. Never a winner.

The World of the News in pictures! X-rated excuse for news
And now Time itself - dressed in pink panties.
Thunder but no light'ning.

More money. More bingo. More of the same. More nothing!
Few Guardians of thought.
Independent ideas dead as the cold print of reality.
Shelter us from ourselves.

Hide us from the truth. Keep us quiet. Cover stories
that leaves nothing on trees.
It's there - in black and white. Must be true - to who?
Royal soaps to cleanse a nation of dirty deeds.

Owned by barons - read by the barren. Unimpress-able.
Glib-gossip gourmets.
Newscrapers with empty headlines of opinion in Trivia.
World exclusives of whimsy.

Obituaries of truth and uncovered fact. No creases, pressed
Together in imprint.
Words widowed and wanting. Waste-paper rapers present profit.
Never a dull moment.

Alex N Hay

165

ANGEL HEART

Caress the wishing spirit,
Which flies above me.
Take the sign -
Then cover me with kisses.
Changing your honour,
Would be too desirable.

Lick your wounds now,
Then shake the dust off your soul.
Question the cruel one,
Who never wakes your smile.
The rising moon that shines,
Will alight your beautiful face.

I'm in misery because,
She bares her sadness.
They call the love to me,
Vying for control.
Disappearance follows the
Oaths' holy path.

Writhing in passionate embraces,
Brings to mind the night.
We want mortal salvation,
Can you find the sight?
But my dear Angel Heart,
I have but one thing to say,
We shall never cry and depart!

Jagdeesh Sokhal

NO GREED, NO HATE

In this world of pain and pleasure
Delusion is the cause of trouble
For without it there's no greed,
Without it then no need to hate.
There are no enemies it seems -
They're but components of my dreams.
All must evaporate.

Dissolve and fade away like mist
When the sun comes out,
They've no strength then to resist,
Dispersed and put to rout
When the truth with its light shines
And all's seen so clear.
Divisions seen as unities,
No enemies to fear.

They're forms constructed in my head,
Really not existing,
Figures of an ill-judged hatred,
Obstinate, persisting,
Until the clear light shows us truly
That it's all a sham.
Opposites are seen as purely
Two sides of the same.

All things are known as unity -
Are not separate,
Together joined in amity
So - no greed, no hate.

Cleone Rear

VENUS SPOKE TO ME

As the moon slipped between the clouds,
I wondered at the chalky glow of radiance.
As my eyes became wearisome, I saw dark figures
and the stars acknowledged me in calling light.
Then upon me came a vision of eternal beauty,
and words of a love virus that spins hearts:

Women are the water that flow through the hands of love,
and men the desperate salmon fighting times tide.
Would these two meet in clashing rocks and windy shores
As one knows the other and calls he or she closely.
The slippery days of heartache will shake the mind,
and loves illusion lost in starry nights denies itself.

Would you drop your anchor in shifting sands?
Then be sure footed when you show your heart,
and show it as you might sing in joyful praise,
or dance with the beauty of movement.
And if you should find that special dream of love
then hold it dear as if it were your last embrace.

Stephen Baggs

DO NOT LOOK

Do not look at me when I am dancing:
The steps I take are often out of time.
The rhythm of my movements is too subtle
For you to sense the beat that's only mine.

Do not watch my lips when I am talking:
The words you read there can't be understood.
Their sense is lost beneath the need of speaking.
To pay attention won't do any good.

Do not watch my eyes when I am smiling:
They tell you nothing of what goes on inside -
Their laughter is a mood that's quickly passing.
Their sadness is the truth I try to hide.

Do not look at me when I am singing:
The notes you hear are always out of key.
The melody is not of my own making
And does not bare the soul that's really me.

You will never find me just by looking
At what you see reflected in your eyes.
The image is an unreal substitution
For that which deep within me really lies.

K Douglas

GEORGINA

Thou, a waltz of wonder, fresh with amorous passion
That alters not.
Amongst the glades I wander, falling like spineless
Grass -
So carried upon an air of gentleness that forever is
You.
'Tis said clusters of roses are the creation of fine
Eloquent craftsmen,
What then brings forth such tempestuous lips, always
Within my heart -
Once kissed?
I looked, and there was my soul passing amidst white
Pillars -
Paved with the melody of your beauty.
As a quiet magic, you walk the paths of dreamy scenes
Of pleasure,
Here stand I, risen high in love -
At the sound of your name.

M Robinson

TODAY

Today is Saturday and today, I feel fine.
Yesterday was Friday when I felt unreal.
Tomorrow is Sunday: is the day to come?
How will I be, well or ill? Well, wait and see.
What constitutes the well of wellness or
the well of illness? Comparative to what?
To what I used to be, but when, and
when was that a true representation of me.

I walk the corridors keeping to a line
but also I wander letting the line unreel,
unravelling, mindlessly minding not where I roam
in the labyrinth of the unreal reality to be
or not. This is the mind's task and for
that in part created, by imparting that
creation of the real in unreal from the sand-
like drifting dunes of possible times to be.

A P F Duncan

THE QUEEN OF MEMORIES

There's a garden in the back of my mind,
Overgrown now with weeds of guilt.
Strangled by forgotten remorse.
The bluebells ring to call the Queen of Memories,
She who can warm the heart with a smile
Or empty your soul with a lash of her tongue
It's autumn now, the frost bites deep,
I look back to carefree spring,
And pleasurable summer,
I fear the oncoming winter with its chilling tendrils
which numb the body and soul.
The gate used forever to stand open, people free to come and go.
Yet now it is rusted shut, forbidding entry and trapping me with my regrets,
Alone save the weeds and the Queen of Memories.

Kate Duggan

AN INDEPENDENT MAN

He is a man alone
He was right from the start
And yet he is their leader.
He thought things through
He knew, and knew that he knew
And others knew it too.

He could see the consequence
Of actions at a glance,
As a chess player
Can foresee the moves
He watched the clouds gather
And saw imminent disaster.

They didn't want to know
They wouldn't ever listen.
As they hurtled to the brink
They would not stop to think,
And hated in their plight
To know that he was right.

They turned to him for help
In any crisis situation
He didn't want their woes
He didn't - God knows!
But he could see their pain
And bore it once again.

His quiet sensitivity
His consummate integrity
Were more than they could bear.
They raised him to the top,
They could ignore him there
Until they needed him once more.

Janet Hawkes

LAST WINTER

Last winter
When it rained
Lusty dreams
Leaving
Strange stains

All over this haunted house
In places I sometimes . . .
Found myself

Last winter
When the frost
Froze on the fields
Not giving
A toss

I left the world to its fate
And took to bed to . . .
Hibernate

And
Last winter
When I drew
Mind pictures
Of summer love
Between me and you

I sadly sat the season out
It was nothing really
To write about.

Justin Coe

THE MEEK SHALL INHERIT

They came with blue berets and all the world was full of praise
for they would make the fighting cease
and afterwards there would be peace.
The emerald flag with Islams' crescent
with crude carved cross of Coptic peasant -
common symbols in the long food queue
that shuffles nearer to the soup-pots two by two
- a helpless line of widows and their waifs
and outstretched bony hands of orphan wraiths.
May some or other God make them believe
it's better to give than to receive,
and to the warlord who is far from meek,
these starveling mites must turn the other cheek;
while he waved away the felons of his murderous band,
and with the other, shook the UN Colonel's hand.
When the cease-fire stopped the dying
you still could hear the mourners crying.
But rejoice! for now there's peace!
Until the Blue Berets go home,
Next week.

John Burnside

ECHOES OF THE PAST

The gentle ripples on the water, slowly fade away.
The narrow boat moves gently on, with time to watch the day drift by;
To see the rainbow coloured wings of the Demoiselle dragonfly.
Rushes, by the water's edge, sucked low as we move on.
A willow tree, its branches dip, like grazing cattle, drink their fill
From marshy banks, where intertwined with foxgloves,
The rosebay willowherb grows on, its beauty undisturbed.
Rosehips in full flower would seem to herald winter's store;
And elderflower and hawthorn, their flowering almost o'er.
And in the early morning light, the dew soaked gossamer is bright
With tiny, single diamond beads, stretched like thread, between the reeds.
And as the fading daylight yields to sunset o'er the hill,
The lengthening shadows cast an eerie presence on the mill.
Crumbling ruins, ivy clad, mock modern ways of man.
Her years of toil are over, but her memories far out-span
The test of time. The silent mill.
A liquid sky; a night so still.
The last faint cry of bleating sheep.
The evening falls,
And day must sleep.

Linda J Bodicoat

TOUCHED BY THE TIDE

There's a lake on an island,
In a sea of my mind.
There's a violent storm brewing,
Acting as a sign.
Sweeping across the island,
Flattening all life.
Stirring up the calm lake,
Causing untold strife.
A hurricane of madness,
Rage and riot like my soul.
My thoughts are ripped to pieces,
And in my heart is torn a hole.
There's a love that's swept away,
By the wind of consciousness.
There's a violent storm subsiding,
Uncovering my loneliness.
Peace begins to settle,
Washed up on the shore.
I watch the gentle tide,
And I don't cry anymore.
There's a bird in a tree,
On the island in the sea.
There's a gathering of clouds,
Slowly forming above me.
A dawning of a conscience,
Beginning to take flight.
The old story has ended sadly,
And a new start beckons - into the light . . .

Barnaby Jones

THE MAGIC BOX

I will put in the box
a feather from the wing of a pigeon
and the memories of an African elephant.
I will put in this box
the most precious thing of a soldier about to die
and the ear of Van Gogh.
I will put in a single crystal clear tear
and a drop of rain.
Materials of the finest quality will go in,
as well as a solid gold bullet and the cry of a baby.
My box is made of light;
it has no lid, but its corners are made of dreams.
I will travel to the boundaries of space and never come back.
I will turn it into a house and live in it for ever,
And when I am dead it will be my grave.

Alexander Evangelidis

ALL THINGS

She makes daisy-chains in the graveyard,
is the shopkeeper in an improvised shop
on top of the fridge
with plastic cash-register and borrowed coins,
painstakingly in a brand-new book
notes down the life-history of dogs she knows.

She flies into a frenzy
when I mention the late hour,
frantic for her little games to remain undisturbed
in her dream of things.

I don't drag her away from her play,
indulge daisy-chains in the graveyard
cling fearfully to her fantasies a while longer.

Alan Hardy

THE PARTNERSHIP

Still.
After years of sweat and toil,
Of sleepless nights and babies' cries.
Still.
Still, after agonies of yes, and no,
Of can, and can't
And tear-soaked sheets
And broken toys.
Still, years on, after whims and sulks
And party hats and shattered knees.
Still,
With loft-space bulging,
Tutus, boomerangs and piano-score.
Still, after ball games DJS
Beermats and scrolls
And occasional telephone calls.
Here, you and I, still
Together.
Amazing how fleeting it all was.
Amazing how happy and traumatic
It all was.
Amazing, that,
Throughout it all, the hell and the fury
Here, together, wiser, older
Are we
Still.

Sandra Fraser

AND WHAT SHALL BE YOUR TOMBSTONE?

If I were the mason
I wouldn't choose the radon-bearing granite
That took your life away,
But white, white marble,
Outstanding and attractive
On the dullest, wildest day.

If I were the artist
I wouldn't choose the usual signs
O death's triumph over life,
But bold, bold pictures
Of a happy, caring man
With pretty children and a wife.

If I were the writer
I wouldn't write the usual facts
Of when and why you're gone,
But a clear, clear message
That you were loved and special
And your magic lingers on.

Madge Twiston

A CARDINAL SILENCE

The hand can dance,
dance all it likes;
I hate the hand,
its scaly silver
fish-grease coat,

its jittered nails
that squall and chap
in a blankness that's
as wracked as
wounds.

I loathed its paleness
long before it held
this pen in days gone
dim, grudged its chalky
knuckles' crack

in the goading,
gouging noiseless;
growing now
like a grope
in daylight,

thunder's
gathering slap.

David Jones

DREAMSCAPE

In the doldrums of my mind
Reality is far behind
But eternity lies over yonder sea
Where shafts of moonlight dance with glee
And fish like rays of sunshine dart
Through the valleys of the heart
The warmth of a summer day laps against driftwood castles
And cliffs like hard worn faces strut
The oyster shells like coffers shut
To hide their ivory white fruit
Like the pirate guards his loot
I lay upon the beach so white
When stars like jewels light up the night
A lonely moment I can steal
In fantasies which seem so real
The pleasures of a tranquil stream
Where spritefull sand like stardust gleams
White horses and warriors of the deep
Guide me through my turbulent sleep
The roaring waves fiercely advance
And rain clouds assume their evil stance
Bullets of water plummet down
Easing the deserts displeased frown
Life begins again like spring's young shoots
The singing of the birds and the elm spreading roots
Time again to leave the dream
And the place I hope I'll one day see.

Sarah Nason

FUNGI - ONE

Two golden spheres
were cunningly joined
and edged with black frills.
A small central hole
was filled with insects.
The indentations,
like fingered pressure,
caused shadows to form
in yellow ochre.
Satin on pale silk.
As the torn lips curled
a view from under
caught the eager eye.
The touch of a shoe
toppled its balance.
Slivers of sooty black
stacked by each other
like charred playing cards
waiting to be dealt
by an unseen hand.
Eyes had to follow
to where rain or frost
jagged its perfection,
then to the column
of creamy white flesh
fiercely embedded
in the soot black blades.
Its flush of orange
dared the inner voice
the whisper of *death*.

Pearl Foy

BORNE ON THE WIND

You lived long
When the hills were green
And summer songs were sang
When the sun always shined
Upon the heather's golden leaves
Nature's life seemed to be borne on the wind
Blowing over hillocks and rocky mountains
Stemmed with ageing legends young and old.

The pale blue sky,
With flowing silk clouds
Shaped by memories of loving tears
Pass over, carried by the winds of time
And the wings of the sea birds it brings
Hear them calling and calling
The song of the sea
Through the air of yester year.

Moving shadows on the lowly ground
Crowding the imagination of a sleepy mind
While you hum a melody quietly to yourself
Of old desired love
That burnt out all those years ago,
Now it seemed it was falling amongst Autumn leaves
All dried out and dying,
But someday you hoped
That you would be borne on the wind
Like nature's life.

Justin Mason

MYSTICAL UNION

From heaven He came and sought her
to be His holy bride.
The trusting place, the place apart
the bearing of the sacred heart.
He found her in Gethsemane.

They fled him in Gethsemane.
His vision they denied.
They did not watch. They did not pray.
But took his bride. And stole away.

Two thousand years, through anguished tears,
She pleads them, 'Find my garden.'
They lead her up a path apart.
She aches to find that lonely heart.
They've taken her to Eden.

Douglas B MacKay

UNTITLED

So strange, and stranger it could never be
That man can make a virtue of his way
Of profiting, make figures in a book
The end of striving life, its endless play.

So strange we see our starving kind and pass
With little noise 'so must be' we do prate,
'It will cost a pain to change, so let alone
And God will soothe their pain and hear their hate'

The skies of blue may wrap the earth with joy,
And fresh green leaves the land a beauty give,
But yet there's lean and wasted human lives.
And joyless children in our towns do live.

C W Lovell

THE HARD FACTS OF WAR

When can we gaze into each other's eyes; and
Feel our love radiating through our whole being?

Perhaps; in a short while.
Only now you must leave
To travel into a world
Of stereo-types.
Where everyone plays a life-like game
Of tin soldiers.
Learning to kill like automatons,
Convincing the mind
It is a glorious thing
To die for one's country.
How many have died in the past?
One-thousand-seven-hundred and sixty-two
Human beings,
Once clad in camouflage suits
Lie side by side; dead,
Like the tin soldiers on the shelf,
Only they are in boxes; and
The once bright-eyed Major
Who loved to play at imitating war,
Telling his troops of its glory,
Now lies alongside his comrades
In some foreign field, far from home.

The penalty is paid, nothing is said,
Of the lonely and depressed left behind,
Now only left to dream . . . to wish
They can gaze into their loved one's eyes,
Like how it used to be,
Before learning to fight became a reality.

Catherine Ross

LIVING FOR THE MOMENT

We wait in breathless expectation,
Round the smoking conflagration.
A black and silent dormancy,
Erupts, now, into ecstasy.
Behold its parabolic rise,
Zip up the dark November skies,
Exploding to expel its pleasure,
In a flash too transient to measure.
A thousand starlets glow and die,
As milliseconds pass us by.
A single spark delays descending,
Teasing, lingering, then ending.
A mere moment from its birth,
Bereft of life, it falls to Earth.

Margaret Hockney

THE GIFT OF EYES AND SIGHT

Not as a scientific experiment -
but just to test a gift from heaven sent
I wondered how it would be,
if for some reason, I could not see.
Getting up was the same as before.
I fell out of bed and straight on the floor.
Groping in the darkness, looking for the light
I remembered for me, it was out of sight.
As the hours passed and the day progressed
I found myself becoming frustrated and even depressed
Relying on others and memories from the past
my independence was vanishing fast.
Without my eyes, I was vulnerable and a target for abuse.
My gift from heaven, I would never again misuse.

Lilian Blackwell

INFORMATION

We hope you have enjoyed reading this book - and that you will continue to enjoy it in the coming years.

If you like reading and writing poetry drop us a line, or give us a call, and we'll send you a free information pack.

Write to

Poetry Now Information
1-2 Wainman Road
Woodston
Peterborough
PE2 7BU.